WOMEN:
WHERE WOULD THE WORLD BE WITHOUT YOU?

J. P. Vaswani

Published by:
GITA PUBLISHING HOUSE
Sadhu Vaswani Mission,
10, Sadhu Vaswani Path,
Pune - 411 001, (India).
gph@sadhuvaswani.org

Women:Where Would The World Be Without You?
© 2013, J.P. Vaswani
ISBN: 978-93-80743-73-8

DADA VASWANI'S BOOKS
Visit us online to purchase books on self-improvement, spiritual
advancement, meditation and philosophy. Plus audio cassettes, CDs,
DVDs, monthly journals and books in Hindi.
www.dadavaswanisbooks.org

Printed by:
MEHTA OFFSET PVT. LTD.
Mehta House,
A-16, Naraina Industrial Area II,
New Delhi - 110 028, (India).
info@mehtaoffset.com

WOMEN:
WHERE WOULD THE WORLD
BE WITHOUT YOU?

J. P. Vaswani

GITA PUBLISHING HOUSE
PUNE, (India).
www.dadvaswanisbooks.org

Books and Booklets by Dada J.P. Vaswani

Dedication:

To

Beloved Mother,

Smt. Krishna P. Vaswani –

a woman of faith and courage,

of simplicity, sweetness and strength –

who, out of the fullness of an

understanding heart,

permitted me to offer myself at the

feet of my loving Master,

Sadhu Vaswani,

at a time when she needed me the most.

Ma, India hath need of mothers like thee!

J. P. Vaswani

CONTENTS

Women fashion the soul of a nation. They hold
fast on to tradition and so sustain
the continuity of a people.

- Sadhu Vaswani

Author's Preface

Time and again, I have had the opportunity to recall the stirring words of my beloved Gurudev, Sadhu Vaswani: "The woman-soul shall lead us upward on!"

I share his view that the future, indeed, belongs to women. I believe in his conviction that it is women who will take up the task of building the civilisation of the future, based on those great ideals of simplicity, sympathy, selfless service, silent sacrifice and spiritual aspiration. It is women who will have the *shakti* to rebuild the shattered world in the strength and integrity of their intuition, dedication and spirit of commitment.

Gurudev Sadhu Vaswani was, in many ways, the initiator of a great liberating movement which aimed to give women their rightful place in society, in the hidebound and conservative world of undivided India, as early as the 1920s. The women of Sind were the first beneficiaries of this quiet, non-violent revolution that he spearheaded.

Feminism, women's liberation and the empowerment of women have become much used, almost clichéd expressions now. In the days before the word 'feminism' was even coined, Gurudev Sadhu Vaswani did everything he could to break the shackles of superstition and hidebound 'customs' that had kept Sindhi women restricted and confined for centuries. He offered the *purdah*-clad, kitchen-bound women of Sind, *spiritual liberation* in the true sense of the term. Indeed, I would say that he was the initiator of a unique women's movement, which focussed on the spiritual strength of women. How many of you who read this book in the second decade of the twenty-first century will believe me if I tell you that this great liberating movement began in a *satsang*?

His *Sakhi Satsang,* a spiritual association of women formed for the purpose of helping them to realise their true potential, enabled many women to become decision-makers for the first time in their personal lives – by the very act of voluntarily joining his *satsang*. It would be no exaggeration to say that he inducted Sindhi women into what had until then been the domain of men – the *practice* of religion in the true sense.

He spoke out against the *purdah* as also against the deadly custom of *deti-leti* (dowry). At the same time, he was also aware of the dangers of excessive 'modernism', warning women against aping western fashions blindly. He encouraged them to cultivate the virtue of simplicity in their dress and in their daily life.

The *Sakhi Satsang* was quite revolutionary in its spiritual, social, cultural and economic impact on Sindhi women, if one were to consider the Movement in all its aspects. For the first time, women learnt about economic independence, accountability and trust, when they were given the management of *Sakhi* Stores. They took their first steps on the path of self-reliance, outside the secure confines of their own homes.

At the *Sakhi* Conference organised by him for their benefit, they had the chance to make themselves heard on matters concerning themselves; on social evils like dowry, child marriage and exploitation. Gurudev Sadhu Vaswani's *Seva Ashram* opened a new world to women who wished to tread the spiritual path. Above all, he emphasised the spiritual *shakti* of women, exclaiming aloud to the male-dominated society, "The woman soul shall lead us upward, on!"

Gurudev Sadhu Vaswani's contribution to women's education was equally significant. The MIRA Movement in Education which he founded in Hyderabad-Sind set new standards for value-based education which emphasised character building and cultivation of the soul. The Mira Movement was, first and foremost, an educational movement exclusively devoted to the development of woman power. His ideal of the triple training of the head, the hand and the heart added a new dimension to the education for girls.

This book is my humble tribute to the great visionary and prophet of modern India, Gurudev Sadhu Vaswani, whose faith in the woman-soul was tremendous. It is also an expression of my deep appreciation of that wonderful half of the human population – our women, our mothers, sisters and daughters – who alone are capable of touching life at its very core.

In my own way, I like to think that women are superior to men; for *he* is only a part of *she*; *male* is only a part of *female*; and, needless to say, *man* is but a fraction of *woman*!

I offer for your reflection the beautiful words of Gurudev Sadhu Vaswani:

A New World is in the making.

The man-made world has proved to be a broken, bleeding world.

Man has blundered badly, for man has believed in force. Even marriage at one time, was marriage by capture.

Man has had his chance. Masculine mentality has blundered.

Now woman gets her chance. She is called upon to build a New World.

She is a symbol of *shakti* in the Hindu scriptures. And *shakti* is not force. *Shakti* is integration.

Today, disintegration is setting in. A woman is the centre of social integration... Our homes must move in a new atmosphere of the simple life; else they will break up for they cannot stand the strain of this heavy drain...

The woman-soul has the *shakti* to rebuild the shattered world in the strength of her intuitions, her purity, her simplicity, her spiritual aspirations, her sympathy and silent sacrifice.

The woman-soul will lead us upward on!

J.P. Vaswani

SITA

Sita is the epitome of the ideal Indian woman, as daughter, as wife and mother. As the wife of Sri Rama, who is an incarnation of Lord Vishnu, she is an aspect of His Divine Consort, Lakshmi. But this does not mean she is superhuman, and therefore, an impractical, unachievable role model for us: one of the striking features of Sri Rama *Avatara* was that the Lord subjected Himself and His wife to human limitations, human obligations, human restrictions and adversities – and still upheld the highest morals and virtues, against all odds. Sita therefore, is an outstanding example of virtue, fortitude, forbearance and inner strength.

Daughter of a great king, Janaka, Sita was married to a prince and was expected to become, in her turn, a great queen. But Divine Will ordained it otherwise – just as it does to other mortals. When her husband voluntarily took up exile from his father's kingdom, Sita followed him to *vanvaas* (life in the forest) for fourteen years. She *could* have chosen to stay behind – but she believed that a wife's rightful place was beside her husband – a splendid gesture in favour of the sanctity of the marriage bond.

The young couple's sojourn in the forests was austere, simple and devoid of all luxury – but it was, nevertheless, idyllic and blissfully serene, until the unthinkable happened, and Sita was abducted by the demon, Ravana.

What ensued was utter misery for the couple – Sita's incarceration, isolation and enforced separation from her husband. That Sita survived it, was testimony to her fortitude, her patience and her undying faith.

Many modern scholars and critics regard Sita as

a symbol of the abject subjugation and degradation of women: their argument is that she allowed herself to be put through the ordeal of fire to 'prove' her virtue; she allowed herself to be exiled from her husband's home and kingdom to help establish her husband's integrity as a perfect ruler; and she surrendered all her rights as queen and wife to bring up her sons all alone – without a protest!

I look at Sita a little differently. The life of Sri Rama and Sita were Divinely ordained to show us how exacting and arduous it is to follow the highest moral standards in private life and the highest ethical standards in public life. To construe such lofty and noble conduct in superficial modern terms is to do grave injustice to our great epics and the deeply symbolic lives our Divine incarnations lived. True, a modern woman may not act or react with Sita's forbearance and fortitude – in this sense, she is not what we may call a 'role-model'; but she does represent an ideal that we may attempt to emulate, to the best of our ability!

Selflessness, forgiveness, the capacity to endure suffering for the sake of the ultimate good – are these not the qualities of all saints and saviours? We would do well to remember too, that Sita was the daughter of Mother Earth – an aspect of Bhumata. Does the earth not show us the same forbearance that Sita displayed?

In her love, loyalty, faith, courage, patience and the firm conviction to stand up for what she believed to be right, Sita is a star among women!

A Word About This Book...

This is not just a book by a man about women.

It is a tribute to womanhood and women everywhere.

It is a recognition that one half of humanity are my equals, perhaps my betters in human traits that make us really good human beings.

I am aware that they are different, but they are nevertheless my fellow human beings, my sisters.

Let me begin with the story of a princess of yore, who was a rebel, a pathbreaker, a woman who lived life on her own terms and achieved her life's goal against all odds.

Can you guess who she is?

She was not a scholar or a prophet; yet she was a social reformer. She was not a rationalist or atheist; yet she shattered narrow traditions. She was born, brought up and married into the most conservative and patriarchal family; yet she had the courage of conviction to stand up for what she believed in. She lived in an age when women had no identity of their own, except as daughters, mothers and wives; yet she broke away from hidebound conventions to create a unique identity for herself; as a free spirit, as a pure soul, as a trailblazer...

Chhand gayi kul ki aan kaa kari hai koi...

I renounced the reputation of my lineage, so what can anyone do to me?

Some of you probably recognised those immortal words.

Yes, she was none other than Mira! The princess who turned into a wandering minstrel, the singing saint, beloved of thousands of Indians, the devotee of Sri Krishna who turned her back on wealth and pomp and power, to seek Liberation and Union with the Lord! Her very name is dear to all of us, the devotees of Gurudev Sadhu Vaswani, for Gurudev chose her as a role model for the woman-soul; he chose to name his new Education Movement after her. Let me begin this account of Mira's life with his own words:

> Four centuries and a half ago, was born, in a village in Mewar, that spiritual genius, the great singer of the love of God – Saint Mira. She lives in the heart of India. Her songs are so unspeakably rich in the wisdom of the Spirit! Her life was so simple and so sublime!

> "God's saints are shining lights," said a mystic. From the Himalayas to Cape Comorin, from Karachi to Calcutta, Mira is to many a "shining light". The secret of her light is devotion (*bhakti*) to Sri Krishna.

> In Rajasthan, in Gujarat, and in North India, her songs are still sung in many homes, the central note of the song being – "I abandon all to Thee, O Lord! To Thee I surrender all I am!"

I abandon all to Thee, O Lord!

How many of us can say that – and mean every word?

She made up her mind about what she wanted to do at a very early age: she never ever swerved from her ideal.

Morey to Giridhar Gopal doosro na koyi...

She wanted to devote her life to the Lord; they married her off as a child bride; she became a young widow; they actually expected her to commit *sati,* burning herself alive on her husband's funeral pyre, as was the tradition among Rajput queens. As an alternative to this, they had thought that she would live in seclusion and isolation. She defied all restrictions and regulations.

Instead of following traditional norms imposed on her by a feudal society, Mira took to a life of ardent worship, becoming one of the leading forces of the great *Bhakti* Movement, which was then sweeping all over medieval India. She openly referred to herself as the Lord's slave, the spouse of Sri Krishna. Like so many saints associated with the *Bhakti* Movement, she ignored petty, parochial divisions of gender, class, caste and religious boundaries, and spent time caring for the poor. Her true devotion, her Divine songs and the sheer spiritual magnetism of her *bhakti,* drew many followers to her temple. They thought that the young princess was the very embodiment of piety. They became Krishna *bhaktas* themselves, and gathered in large numbers to join her *kirtan* and *pujas* at the shrine. Her popularity among the common people grew from more to more. She too, felt she was one of them; for how can there be rich and poor, high and low, prince and pauper, man and woman among the lovers of the Lord? If she was a devotee, so were they; if they were servants of Sri Krishna, so was she. They grew to love her, and she mingled with them freely. At times, overcome by her intense devotion, she would even go out on to the streets, stringing her *tanpura,* and dancing in ecstatic piety.

She was subjected to severe persecution and mental torture; her sister-in-law actually tried to poison her. She bore it all in patience, with undaunted courage. In every difficulty and crisis that she faced, her only support and solace was her devotion to Sri Krishna.

There is one important phase of her life that is of special interest to this book, which I would like to highlight here.

Gurudev Sadhu Vaswani tells us, that it is ever the fate of those who aspire to meet the Lord, that they must face loneliness; they must tread their chosen path all alone.

Alone, Mira leaves Chittor, in the darkness of the night. Alone, she moves out, this Rajput princess, who is truly heroic at heart, firm in her devotion for Sri Krishna. As Gurudev Sadhu Vaswani puts it, this is indeed a difficult period in her life – difficult, but blessed. She walks the way of quest, her heart crying out again and again, "Where, O, where art Thou, Beloved?"

Moving along the pilgrim way, she visits shrine after shrine, until she reaches Brindavan. Here she finds a thousand temples dedicated to her dear Sri Krishna. For it was here that He grew up, here that He tended His cows, here that He played the flute, capturing the hearts of the *gopas* and *gopis,* His playmates and beloved companions. Mira's heart is filled with ecstasy!

In Brindavan, she comes to the temple wherein is located the *ashram* of Jiva Goswami, the great disciple of Chaitanya Mahaprabhu. Mira is anxious to have his *darshan;* standing at the gates of the temple, she sends word that she wishes to pay her respects to the Goswami.

Back comes the prompt reply, "I never meet women!"

Mira smiles. "Foolish me!" she exclaims. "In my ignorance I thought that Sri Krishna was the only Male – the *Purushottama* – in Brindavan, while the rest of us were all His *gopis*. Now I know, that He has a peer, a rival, who also considers himself a male in Brindavan!"

Jiva Goswami is unnerved by the statement. He realises that it is no ordinary *bairagin* who stands at his gate. She is a supreme devotee of the Lord. He rises from his seat and rushes out to open the gates of his *kutiya*. With great reverence and admiration he ushers Mira inside. She has opened his eyes to the truth that there can be no bias, no discrimination among the devotees of the Lord.

To the generation that believes Men are from Mars and Women are from Venus, I humbly refer the shining example of Mira.

Many of us continue to believe, even today, that a woman's place is in the home, in the kitchen, two steps behind a father or a husband, submissive, ever obeying instructions and orders, never asserting her identity. Any woman who breaks away to forge her own image is ostracised and viewed with suspicion. And yet, despite this conviction that she is weak and helpless, the most atrocious forms of violence are perpetrated against her! What is worse, some people even insist that if she is abused and molested, it is all her fault! She is the one to be blamed!

With Mira to inspire and guide us, let us set out to right the wrong, at least in our attitudes and our way of thinking. Let us attempt to understand woman and what she really represents.

SECTION I

TO RIGHT THE WRONG....

Why Are Some of Us More Equal Than Others?

We have heard it said again and again: all of us are equal in the eyes of God; all of us are born free; all of us should enjoy equal rights...

The UN Declaration of Human rights states this emphatically:

> All human beings are born free and equal in dignity and rights. They are endowed with reason and conscience and should act towards one another in a spirit of brotherhood.

Gender Inequality denies this basic premise. It is a gap that divides men and women, keeping women at an artificially created (man made) disadvantage, by denying them equal opportunities in health care, education, empowerment and economic attainments.

Equality is not a concept of sameness. We are all gloriously unlike each other, refreshingly different in our mental and physical make-up. But the differences should be celebrated, not discriminated.

A sister said to me, "When girls are born, we dress them in pink; and the discrimination begins right there!"

At home, sons are given greater freedom; sons get to keep the landed property; men eat their dinners and lunches first; sons get to study what they choose; sons have their say in all matters...

At the workplace, there is income disparity; there is the glass ceiling, the invisible roof beyond which a woman's career cannot grow; there is harassment from superiors and colleagues; there is lack of care and facilities; there are opportunities denied...

In the family, mothers cook and clean and care for the children; fathers go out to work and are breadwinners; housework is not shared equally; women are expected to stretch their time and efforts to do all that is expected of them, falling into the double shift syndrome...Even when women earn more than men, they are still primary caregivers. A recent report suggests that women who work outside the home often put an extra 18 hours a week doing household or childcare related chores as opposed to men who average 12 minutes a day in childcare activities.

In the rural areas of developing countries like India, the face of gender inequality is even more ugly; women and girls even starve so that the males of the house can eat well; hard and laborious tasks like fuel gathering and fetching water from great distances are left to the women and girls; young girls are taken out from school to look after their younger siblings and cook for the family; child marriages, forced marriages and marriages of convenience are still rampant.

Gender inequality occurs due to prejudiced treatment leading to discrimination and sexism. It varies from place to place and is determined by race, culture, economic status and even politics. True, some men are also victims of such inequality; but as UN experts say, "Discrimination against women is an entrenched, global pandemic". In some third world countries, rape and violence against women are used as tools of war!

Even in the world's most powerful country, the US, women are more likely than men "to live in poverty, earn less money for the same work, are more likely to be victims of intimate partner violence and rape, and have less of a political voice".

How can we create a more fair and equitable society which does not discriminate against one half of its own people?

Worse Than Murder!

Here are some facts and figures that should make Indians hang their heads in shame: the BBC recently reported that more than ten million female foetuses have been illegally aborted in India. Researchers for the *Lancet* journal based in Canada and India stated that 500,000 girls were being lost annually through sex selective abortions.

The horror of taking a life away before it is even born upon earth... the unspeakable tragedy of mothers, fathers, grandmothers, grandfathers, aunts and uncles colluding to kill a child that is heir to the family...and doctors who have affirmed the Hippocratic oath assisting this process...

Some of us are laboring under the false delusion that such 'barbaric practices' are confined to rural areas and primitive, illiterate rural communities. We cannot be more mistaken. It is happening, even as we speak, in educated, affluent upper class urban homes, where daughters are not wanted.

When infant daughters are born to educated women, her husband and in-laws don't bother to come and see the baby in the nursing home. Some women are unceremoniously abandoned by the husbands for having committed the unpardonable act of giving birth to a daughter. If the girl babies are brought home, they are either forcibly poisoned or abandoned at the insistence of the powers-that-be...

A report based on the 2011 Census tells us that the rate at which the unborn female child is killed amounts to killing off 10,00,000 girls a year. The long term adverse effect of this pernicious practice is that the gender ratio is beginning to drop alarmingly!

When will we realise that the girl child is not meant to be a prey to our killing instincts?

Her Safest Sanctuary?

Physical violence: hitting, kicking, shoving, pushing, slapping, throwing objects at the victim...

Emotional violence: verbal abuse, bullying, ridiculing, insulting, intimidating, threatening, neglecting, starving or locking up a victim...

Psychological violence: humiliating, alienating, isolating, controlling, restraining, undermining the self-esteem and self-confidence of the victim...

Dear readers, I am not referring to medieval systems of torture; I am referring to a recurring phenomenon of the 20th and 21st centuries: namely, domestic violence.

All that has been referred to above, happens within the four walls of that sacred space that we call a *griha* or home.

If I seem to refer to reports repeatedly, it is not to take refuge in statistics, but to bring home to you the magnitude of the problem.

We are told that 3.3 million children witness domestic violence each year in the US alone. If you project that figure on to the world population, you can say without exaggeration that at least a billion children must be doing so worldwide.

Most of the perpetrators of domestic violence are men – sadly, fathers and husbands.

According to psychiatrists and sociologists, domestic violence arises out of a need for power and control of one partner over the other. An abuser will use various tactics of abuse (some of them listed above) in order to establish and maintain control over the partner. Unfortunately, these behaviour patterns are often addictive, and lead to a vicious cycle of abuse or violence. Worst of all, it has led to reciprocal violence, in which women are being implicated increasingly, often taking out their anger and powerlessness on children. But the fact remains that women are the worst victims of domestic violence.

Experts tell us that when a boy grows up seeing his father assault his mother, he starts to accept such behaviour and imitates the same.

The fear, shame, anger, guilt and violence involved in these cases has meant that we still remain in the dark about many implications of domestic abuse.

The UN Declaration on the Elimination of Violence against Women (1993) states that "violence against women is a manifestation of historically unequal power relations between men and women, which has led to domination over and discrimination against women by men and to the prevention of the full advancement of women, and that violence against women is one of the crucial social mechanisms by which women are forced into a subordinate position compared with men."

What hope do women have when their safest sanctuary turns into a terror camp?

Daughters Are Not For Sale!

Streedhan (literal meaning: women's wealth) was an ancient and highly respectable practice, which ensured that the daughters of a family got their fair share of ancestral property in the form of gold and silver, while landed property stayed with the family, unfragmented. Perhaps some people may argue that this practice was in itself discriminatory, as land is still the most prized and valuable asset, and women are denied hereditary rights to it. In a society and culture which regards a daughter as *paraya dhan* (another's property) such discrimination is perhaps inevitable.

Streedhan included all material assets, jewellery and utensils gifted by her parents to a bride at the time of her wedding. It was always given voluntarily, never demanded or forced. It also remained the exclusive property of the woman and neither her husband nor his family had any rights over it.

Thus this form of 'dowry' that started off as a practice to give away presents to the departing daughter, in the form of a few resources to begin her new married life, slowly assumed monstrous proportions and turned into a social evil. Dowries began to be demanded, then became extortions, and parents and daughters became hapless victims. Brides were expected to bring in "gifts" regardless of their personal willingness or their parents' capacity. Lengthy lists were prepared and sent to the girl's house before the wedding. And if the demands were not met, weddings were cancelled to the enormous embarrassment and even shame of the girl's family. Thus began the trauma of daughters, who were regarded as a drain on the parents' resources, and therefore to be avoided at all costs through sex-determination tests and illegal abortions.

But the worst part of the story is this: not satisfied with the preliminary acquisitions at the wedding, the bridegroom's parents continued their extortion demands; and when their greed could no longer be appeased, the heinous practice of dowry deaths began to happen with sickening regularity, all over the country. Either the tortured brides committed suicide, or their vicious in-laws burnt them to death and reported that a stove in the kitchen had burst accidentally and killed their dear one!

Even today, this inhumanity continues to flourish. Soon after the marriage, some families start demanding more dowry from the girl's parents. If there are ten thousand cases filed every year, thousands more go unreported, while the fury of greed continues to grow unabated.

It is not that the government has been inactive in this matter: but its ordinances and legislations have proved to be ineffective. Demand for dowry is today a cognizable offence. A groom demanding dowry can be criminally prosecuted. But the perpetrators of this evil are uncaught, unpunished and therefore unafraid.

When will our people return to the ideals of simplicity, honesty, integrity and sincerity? When will we stop buying and selling our girls as brides?

Defender Or Offender?

An atheist brother, afflicted with the terrible ailments of divisive and bigoted thought wrote to me once: "Inequity and degradation of women are sanctified by the Hindu religion".

I was reminded of the words of Mark Twain: "India is the cradle of the human race, the birthplace of human speech, the mother of history, the grandmother of legend and the great grand mother of tradition." He was obviously referring to the *Sanatana Dharma* of ancient India.

Are we talking about the same country and the same people, you might wonder.

The social evils of India are many; but they are not necessarily Hindu evils.

In this country, until a few centuries ago, women walked long distances, across the length and breadth of the vast subcontinent, on *tirth yatras* to Ganga, Yamuna and the sacred Triveni Sangam, as well as on holy pilgrimages to Badrinath in the Himalayas to Rameshwaram in the South; to Jagannath Puri in the East and Dwarka in the west. They walked without fear of molestation or violence; they came to no harm.

But today, we have the dubious distinction of our national capital being labelled "the rape capital of the world". Here is an excerpt from a European newspaper:

More than almost anywhere else, violence against women is a brutal fact of life in the Indian subcontinent. According to official figures cited by Agence France Presse, females were victims in almost 230,000 of the more than 256,000 violent crimes reported in India last year. Just as shocking is the willingness of police, judges and government officials to tolerate attacks on women by blaming victims and excusing offenders.

A BBC report adds fuel to the fire:

Female foetuses are aborted and baby girls killed after birth, leading to an appallingly skewed sex ratio. Many of those who survive face discrimination, prejudice, violence and neglect all their lives, as single or married women.

Trust Law, a news service run by Thomson Reuters, has ranked

India as the worst country in which to be a woman. This, ironically, in a country where the leader of the ruling party, the speaker of the Lower House of Parliament, at least three chief ministers, and a number of sports and business icons are women. It is also a country where a generation of newly empowered young women are going out to work in larger numbers than ever before.

But they are not safe in public places, on the roads, and in public transport. Worst of all, many of them are not even safe at home!

More and more women are becoming educated. But crimes against women are rising too.

With more than 24,000 reported cases in 2011, rape registered a 9.2% rise over the previous year. More than half (54.7%) of the victims were aged between 18 and 30. Most disturbingly, according to police records, the offenders were known to their victims in more than 94% of the cases. Neighbours accounted for a third of the offenders, while parents and other relatives were also involved. Delhi accounted for over 17% of the total number of rape cases in the country.

And it is not rape alone. Police records from 2011 show kidnappings and abductions of women were up by 19.4%, women being killed in disputes over dowry payments by 2.7%, torture by 5.4%, molestation by 5.8% and trafficking by an alarming 122% over the previous year.

What can we do about this national shame?

All In Fun?

Eve teasing is a euphemism, an inoffensive, indirect, mild substitute for a harsh reality on Indian streets – sexual harassment or public verbal/physical molestation of women. It is unfortunately associated with juveniles whose abuse of girls ranges from indecent remarks to offensive insults to actual physical molestation. The 'coy' nature of the term blinds us to its offensive and obscene motives and bullying tactics; it sounds like youthful, innocent fun, but as victims will tell you, it is nothing short of sexual aggression.

Here is an excerpt from Time Magazine, as early as 1960:

> Independent India is discovering social problems undreamed of in Mahatma Gandhi's philosophy. As the caste system and the traditional Hindu family begin to crumble, the barrier between the sexes in India is no longer the formidable fence it used to be. Last week in Agra—where India's two most famous lovers, the Mogul Emperor Shah Jehan and his queen, lie buried under the Taj Mahal—the Indian Youth Association held a solemn seminar about a new kind of problem: the sidewalk dalliance that Indian youth calls "Eve-teasing".

Young men say they do it for 'a bit of fun', to attract the attention of the girls or just to exert pressure over them, to make them feel powerless and scared. But the girls are often traumatised by such behaviour. They often feel degraded and insulted, even humiliated and shamed; they feel complex emotions of anger, disgust, guilt and anxiety; if the teasing persists, they even become demoralized; they try to run away, escape by using a different route, taking alternative transport or withdrawing from the locality; but they are emotionally bruised.

When will our young men learn the ABC of basic courtesy and civility to the opposite sex? When will they learn to see the young women they harass as their own sisters and cousins, whom they should protect and respect?

Are They Really Free?

Slavery was abolished in the West, as late as the nineteenth century, and the effort to declare every human being as a 'self-owner' soon led to a similar movement for women's rights in Europe. Originally, they campaigned for women's suffrage and equal rights. But later, they evolved into the first wave feminists, determined to bring about cultural and social changes in a patriarchal society.

Why are we so nervous when women demand freedom?

For many women, freedom means walking, using public places like libraries, restaurants, cinema halls and even roads without fear of sexual assault; this is their basic freedom to exist, live, move without fear; the rest of their freedom components come up after this basic freedom is assured to them.

Many women lament the fact that in India, women are denied the most basic of rights: the right to be born, the right to be fed, to be educated, to go to work, to control their own earnings independently, to inherit property, and even to dress according to their choice.

Just last month, after the impressive display of the Republic Day parade in New Delhi, a very different kind of 'parade' took to the streets of the national capital, marching from Mandi House to Jantar Mantar; theirs was a march for 'Freedom from Fear'.

Worst of all, when women are attacked, abused, molested and raped, we have begun to blame victims. We even go to the extent of saying, "She was dressed in such and such manner; she was being provocative; she crossed the *Laxman Rekha*," etc. No wonder then, that young girls protesting against outdated rape laws carried placards which read: "Don't teach me what to wear; teach your sons not to rape!"

When will we give them true freedom and true respect?

Can This Happen To A Man?

Everyone should be treated with due respect and dignity in the workplace. Although harassment at work is not to be tolerated, it is easier to say this rather than see it practised; for most people do not know how to handle harassment by employers and colleagues.

Harassment is any form of conduct that is unwanted, affecting the dignity of an individual in the workplace. Although it may be related to age, race, disability or any personal characteristic of the individual, everyone agrees that the most offensive form is sexual harassment that is overt or implicit.

The number of working women has been on the increase over the last few decades. And many of them face both discrimination and sexual harassment at work.

Discrimination is rampant especially when women come up for promotion, when they are denied legitimate opportunities for training and advancement, and also when they are denied the opportunity to care for a child or dependent relatives. Many women are also denied benefits like maternity leave and simply told to quit their jobs when they ask for leave.

It is estimated that 50% of women in employment are, or have been, subject to sexual harassment in one form or another. This is not just true of women who work in large offices or in a predominantly male working environment; it also happens to people in any occupation, to any age group and from every community. Sexual harassment can be verbal, non verbal or even physical. In most countries, employers are held to be liable for the actions of their employees that cause offence to another employee at work. All organisations need to adopt what is called a 'zero tolerance' approach to this insidious practice. Here too, the law is in favour of women; as always, the problem is in the implementation and execution.

More often than not, it is freshers out of college, and young women in the early stages of their career who suffer the most. But many of them do not complain for fear of losing their jobs. Some of them suffer in silence and even face disciplinary procedures for non-performance, while they become stressed and ill with the problems they face.

Unfortunately, technology has created new forms of harassment. Offensive emails and obscene downloads have become common in many offices, along with 'dirty' jokes and text messages. And unfortunately, many women labour under the impression that they have to "put up with it all and shut up about it".

Gender parity and pay parity are still far away for working women. Many of them feel that speaking out will only weaken their existing positions.

Can this happen to a man?

The Gift Of Knowledge

Women's illiteracy is still a rampant problem that affects economic development. But it is not just an economic or social problem; it is a deep personal tragedy for women who cannot be truly empowered as they are not educated.

Yes; even in the Twentieth century, discrimination exists in educational opportunities based on a gender bias.

There are unfortunate consequences to this problem: while literate women average 2 children per family, illiterate women give birth to 6–8 children. Thus literacy makes a great difference to the life of a woman and her family.

"Every literate woman marks a victory over poverty," says UN Secretary-General Ban Ki-moon, emphasising the transformative effect that an educated woman will have on both a family and the wider community. "Literate women are more likely to send their children, especially their girls, to school," he adds. "By acquiring literacy, women become more economically self-reliant and more actively engaged in their country's social, political and cultural life. All evidence shows that investment in literacy for women yields high development dividends."

Educated women have more confidence and self-esteem; they take better care of the family's health and their own health; they access medical care when needed; and they are more likely to insist on the education of their daughters and grand-daughters. A literate woman is also better equipped to handle government aid schemes and other financial services, to read and understand agreements and other documents and to keep accurate records and accounts.

Education is one of the most important means of empowering women and girls with the knowledge and skills necessary to understand their rights and to gain the confidence to claim them, so that they may lead fulfilled lives.

Is it not important for governments to invest in women's literacy? Is this not one of the most fundamental and important investments a country can make to benefit both current and future generations?

Space Of Their Own

Nearly a hundred years ago, a distinguished writer, Virginia Woolf wrote an essay, "A Room of One's Own", which became a milestone in the annals of the Women's Movement.

Her argument is simple but profound: it is relative poverty and lack of freedom that prevents women from doing what they want to do. Ms. Woolf is actually making a case for women writers; but her argument applies to all women who have their own personal aspirations. "A woman must have money and a room of her own if she is to write fiction", she argues. To borrow the metaphor from her symbolic title, women must be given their space, to flower and blossom and attain their full potential.

Women need their space. They need the emotional freedom and the opportunity not only to build their lives, but to build their relationships, nurture their families, build their careers and also foster their intellectual, emotional and spiritual development.

When shall we give them their space?

And when shall we sing of our unsung heroines?

SECTION II

THE SONG OF OUR UNSUNG HEROINES

The facts of gender inequality - the restrictions placed on women's choices, opportunities and participation - have direct and often malign consequences for women's health and education, and for their social and economic participation. Yet until recent years, these restrictions have been considered either unimportant or non-existent, either accepted or ignored. The reality of women's lives has been invisible to men. This invisibility persists at all levels, from the family to the nation.

- From the United Nations Population
Fund (UNFPA) Report

Women are supposed to be very calm generally: but women feel just as men feel; they need exercise for their faculties, and a field for their efforts, as much as their brothers do; they suffer from too rigid a restraint, too absolute a stagnation, precisely as men would suffer; and it is narrow-minded in their more privileged fellow-creatures to say that they ought to confine themselves to making puddings and knitting stockings, to playing on the piano and embroidering bags. It is thoughtless to condemn them, or laugh at them, if they seek to do more or learn more than custom has pronounced necessary for their sex.

- Charlotte Bronte

Chapter 1
Second Class Citizens?

When we look around us, the UNFPA Report quoted on the previous page seems unreal. Women occupy positions of respect, dignity and prestige wherever they go: they are employed at every level, from the highest to the lowest, in banks and private companies; they are professors, directors and principals in many educational institutions; some of them enjoy celebrity status as 'stars' and movie actors; many of them are prominent in the glamorous world of fashion and modeling; and then again, they are increasingly occupying positions in emergent sectors like software and technology; they are doctors and nurses in the best hospitals; women entrepreneurs are becoming prominent these days; the NGOs are virtually dominated by women activists; many women also occupy key positions in government; and under the latest system of 'reserved' posts, many cities like Pune and Mumbai now have women mayors!

Where then is the gender inequality that the report talks about?

I am afraid that it does exist, despite the healthy, visible trend I mentioned above. The world is far from being an 'equal' place for men and women, even today. Try and answer a few questions that I ask, and you will admit that this is indeed so.

- From New York to Nice, from New Delhi to Sydney, can a woman feel safe and secure moving about on her own, without a male escort, especially after dark?

- On city roads and motorways, at parking lots and signals, are women drivers treated with the same courtesy and politeness shown to men?

- Are men and women paid equal wages in the unorganised sector?

- Are women ensured equal or even fair participation in the political system?

■ Are women safe from harassment and discrimination at the workplace?

India presents a very ambivalent picture in this regard. On one hand, we proclaim that our women are goddesses: *griha laxmi, shakti, devi* and *mata*. On the other hand, the very notion of gender equality is unacceptable to the psyche of ordinary men. While many women now occupy leadership roles in elite corporations and higher echelons of society, women at the grass root level are still regarded as weaker and inferior to men.

Inaugurating a Seminar on Women's Status in Indian Society, Shri Krishna Kant, former Union Minister and Governor of Andhra Pradesh, once remarked:

"The fact seems to be that there are women's studies, seminars and some activists organisations in the country, but no real women's movement, and no integrated vision of women in Indian society as it should be. We are oscillating between half-knowledge of the past, fascination for the West and incoherent determination of the future!"

Let me tell you right away, I am not a subscriber to the so-called 'battle between the sexes'. I am a believer in the equality of all human beings; in fact, I belong to a lineage, a great tradition that respects the fundamental rights of all living beings. I am dismayed by the tendency of confrontation and opposition as far as women's issues are concerned. In my view, women's empowerment cannot be regarded as a fight between men and women, but rather as a struggle that is part of the assertion of fundamental human rights, the fight of all human beings for dignity and freedom of choice.

As Mahatma Gandhi was often wont to say: "There is no occasion for women to consider themselves subordinate or inferior to man...Woman is the companion of man, gifted with equal mental capacity."

But the question persists: are we giving our women a fair deal? Are we treating them as our equals? Do we treat them on par with the rest of mankind as our fellow human beings?

The UNFPA reported that in 2008, the world reached an "invisible but momentous milestone". For the first time in history, more than half its human population, i.e. nearly 3.3 billion people, were living in urban areas. By 2030, the agency predicted, this figure was expected to swell

THE SUFFRAGETTE MOVEMENT

Did you know that in most Western nations, suffrage or the right to vote was given to women only at the end of World War I? France was a little late, giving women their voting rights in 1944; Switzerland followed, as late as in 1971.

Suffragettes, so called by the *Daily Mail* newspaper, were mostly women from upper and middle-class backgrounds, who were inspired by the writings of John Stuart Mill to spearhead a movement that would encompass mass groups of women fighting for suffrage.

The Movement was at first marred by violence. The Suffragettes burned down churches as the Church of England was against what they wanted; they chained themselves to Buckingham Palace as the Royal Family were seen to be against women having the right to vote; they sailed up the Thames in hired boats and hurled abuse through loud hailers at Parliament when the session was sitting; they attacked politicians as they went to work. Shops in Oxford Street and Golf courses frequented by men were vandalised. And when the activists were arrested and sent to jail, they went on a hunger strike.

Now the government, which had been indifferent to their protests was forced to sit up and take notice. They did not want the women to become martyrs. Prison officials were ordered to force-feed them. When this was condemned as barbaric, they allowed the women to starve until they were weakened to the point of death and threw them out of prison so that they would not die in custody.

The most violent and infamous act associated with the Suffragettes occurred at the June 1913 Derby Meet, when Emily Wilding Davison threw herself under the King's horse, Anmer, as it rounded Tottenham Corner. She was killed; and the Suffragettes had their first martyr.

But her needless, tragic death did more harm than good to the Movement. Most men who were against them began to argue that such violence and aggression were only indicative of women's emotional imbalance and lack of logical thinking capacity. The skeptics posed a simple question — if this is what an educated woman does, what might a lesser educated woman do? How could such women possibly be given the right to vote?

Thankfully, when World War I came, the suffragette leader, Emmeline Pankhurst, urged her members to stop their campaign of violence and support the government and its war effort in every way possible. As it happened, the work done by women was vital for Britain's war effort.

The outcome was also auspicious for the suffragettes. In 1918, the now historical Representation of the People Act was passed by Parliament, giving all women the right to vote.

to almost 5 billion. Many of the new urbanites, it pointed out, would be poor. Their future, the future of cities in developing countries, the future of humanity itself, would all depend very much on decisions made now in preparation for this growth.

Urbanisation, the state of the world's cities and the effects of urban poverty are all matters of concern for population experts. But we are concerned, in this book, about that half of the world's population which has faced discrimination and inequality in towns, villages, cities, developed and developing countries – I refer to our women, our mothers, daughters, sisters and homemakers.

The Millennium Development Goals are aware that 'development' in the true sense of the term cannot be achieved without gender equality.

The Millennium Development Goals (MDGs) are eight goals to be achieved by 2015 that respond to the world's main development challenges. The MDGs are drawn from the actions and targets contained in the Millennium Declaration that was adopted by 189 nations and signed by 147 heads of state and governments during the UN Millennium Summit in September 2000. I was privileged to be a guest of the UN during this historic summit. I still recall the euphoria and the optimism with which these goals were set.

The eight MDGs break down as follows:

* Goal 1: Eradicate extreme poverty and hunger
* Goal 2: Achieve universal primary education
* Goal 3: Promote gender equality and empower women
* Goal 4: Reduce child mortality
* Goal 5: Improve maternal health
* Goal 6: Combat HIV/AIDS, malaria and other diseases
* Goal 7: Ensure environmental sustainability
* Goal 8: Develop a Global Partnership for Development

2015 was the deadline set to accomplish these goals. What is the position now, in 2013?

UNDP reports reveal that in most developing countries, gender inequality is a major obstacle to meeting the MDG targets. In fact, achieving the goals will be impossible without closing the gaps between women and men in terms of capacities, access to resources and opportunities, and vulnerability to violence and conflict.

We are told that four indicators are used to measure progress towards the desired goal of gender equality:

* the ratio of girls to boys in primary, secondary and tertiary education;
* the ratio of literate women to men in the 15 to 24 year-old age group;
* the share of women in wage employment in the non-agricultural sector; and
* the proportion of seats held by women in national parliaments.

On all four indicators, the results have been far from satisfactory.

Gender discrimination may be characterised as the unequal treatment of a person based solely on that person's gender. Traditionally and historically, women have been the victims of such unequal treatment.

Until the early years of this century, women were not entitled to the same rights and privileges as men, even in developed western nations.

Women were not allowed to vote; they were usually required to surrender control of their property to their husbands upon marriage. Their educational and occupational opportunities were severely limited. It was commonly believed that "a woman's place was in the home" – raising children and tending to domestic affairs.

Indian born Nobel Laureate Dr. Amartya Sen identifies as many as seven different types of inequality which afflicts women all over the world:

(1) Mortality inequality: This involves unusually high mortality rates of women and a consequent preponderance of men in the total population.

(2) Natality inequality: Many patriarchal societies show a marked preference for boys over girls; in such conditions, gender inequality can manifest itself not only in the form of hopes, wishes and dreams, but in ugly and cruel practices like sex-determination tests and sex-selective abortions.

(3) Basic facility inequality: This refers to the fact that in many countries, girls are given less opportunity of schooling than boys. There are other deficiencies in basic facilities available to women, varying from encouragement to cultivate one's natural talents to fair participation in rewarding social functions of the community.

(4) Special opportunity inequality: A strong gender bias in higher education and professional training can be observed even in some of the richest countries in the world in Europe and North America.

(5) Professional inequality: In terms of employment as well as promotion in work and occupation, women often face greater handicap than men.

(6) Ownership inequality: In many societies the ownership of property is found to be very unequal. Even basic assets such as homes and land are asymmetrically shared. The absence of claims to property not only reduces opportunities for women, but also makes it harder for women to enter and flourish in commercial, economic and even some social activities.

(7) Household inequality: There are, often enough, basic inequalities in gender relations within the family or the household, which can take many different forms. It is, for example, quite common in

many societies to take it for granted that while men will naturally work outside the home, women could do it if and only if they could combine it with various inescapable and unequally shared household duties. This is sometimes called "division of labour", though women could be forgiven for seeing it as "accumulation of labour".

(Courtesy: Dr. Amartya Sen's Inaugural lecture at the Radcliffe Institute)

New global realities have presented additional hurdles in efforts to end gender inequalities. Women's advocates and government delegates who met at the United Nations in March 2005 to weigh the gains over the last decade described increasingly challenging times. They cited the rise of various forms of religious fundamentalism; a concentration of resources on the war on terror at the expense of poverty reduction; widening gaps between the rich and the poor; increased trafficking of women and children; new wars and conflicts, and violence against refugee and other marginalised women.

May I also humbly submit, that our fight for equality and justice for our sisters must not take us away from the very positive aspects of our culture and tradition that gave dignity and security to women in the family. While we must do everything we can to eradicate the social evils that hamper women's empowerment, we must not permit our agenda to be hijacked by crass commercialism and consumerism, allowing women to be exploited in new and insidious ways. I strongly feel that any attempt to disrupt the family in the name of liberation or empowerment of women will only prove counter productive to their progress and happiness.

Women represent half of the world's population. This double standard for girls and women hurts everyone in society and has a negative impact on economic development. Societies in which women have equal rights are wealthier. These countries prosper more, grow faster and have better governance systems, which are important for growth and development.

Conversely, inequalities between women and men tend to be the largest among the poor, according to *Engendering Development,* a World Bank publication that talks about the importance of gender for development.

In some Indian villages, men are likely to spend a big portion of their income for personal use (such as smoking, drinking, gambling) while the women devote all of their income to family needs (such as food, medical treatment, school fees and children's clothing), according to an Indian study cited in *Voices of the Poor,* a collection of interviews of more than 60,000 poor women and men around the world.

In Africa, where most people earn a living by working in agriculture, women do at least 70% of farm work. Yet they have very little say in how this income gets spent. And when women aren't allowed to make decisions on how to use financial income to help their families, it becomes more difficult to help poor people climb out of poverty, explains Mark Blackden, the World Bank's lead gender specialist for Africa. The situation becomes even more critical in households headed by women. The lack of access to legal, economic and social services often leaves them poorer.

– World Bank Initiative – *You Think*

HELEN KELLER

"Character cannot be developed in ease and quiet," Helen Keller once remarked. "Only through the experience of trial and suffering can the soul be strengthened, ambition inspired, and success achieved."

Helen Keller's life was witness to those words! Her teachers in school and college, her close friends and admirers always marvelled at her confidence and courage. It was indeed remarkable, they felt, that a person who was so severely disabled – she could not hear, speak or see – could reach out to so many people and inspire them.

Helen Keller was born on June 27, 1880, in America. Her father was a Captain in the Civil War. She was born a normal child. She could see and hear. But when she was a year and a half old, she fell very sick. Her parents were afraid that she would not survive. Although she recovered from the illness, it left her unable to see. She would never be able to hear, nor would she ever be able to utter a single word.

As she grew up, this little child was bewildered, traumatised by what had happened to her. Why could she not hear her father and mother's voices or see them? Her condition was similar to that of a wild animal.

Her parents took her to the best doctor in Baltimore. After examining her, the doctor solemnly stated, "Helen will never be able to see and hear. We can do nothing to help her." Dejected, the parents returned home. Helen lived a miserable life.

Her parents sincerely prayed to God to show them the way. Finally, their prayers were answered and a teacher called Annie Sullivan, offered to train Helen.

Annie Sullivan's life was also in a way, unique. She had been through several illnesses and survived them all. She was familiar with pain. So her heart moved out in sympathy to Helen and she resolved to help Helen and bring about a change in her life. Annie started off by writing different words for different things on the child's hand. Helen, in return, started memorising those words. In her autobiography, Helen Keller writes, "The day I could identify things by their name was, indeed memorable... I don't think any one must have ever experienced so much joy." Just a little before her eighth birthday, both her mother and Annie, took Helen to Massachusetts. Helen carried with herself her favourite doll and some books in Braille. When the mother and Annie wanted to rest, Helen would start reading.

Newspapers now started carrying stories about Helen Keller. People were amazed to know how a deaf, dumb and blind child could actually read and communicate. She was now becoming a celebrity.

At the age of 10, Helen had another teacher, whose name was Miss Fuller. She taught Helen how to talk. Helen being intelligent, opened her mouth like her teacher, stuck her tongue out and made her first sound. On the very first day itself, Miss Fuller was successful in teaching her six letters of the English language. Helen practised her speech very sincerely and the day dawned when she could also speak. At the age of 14, Dr. Humason gave Helen special lessons in speaking and reading.

In June 1904, Helen graduated from Radcliffe College, where she had been elected Vice President of her class. Now Helen Keller took more speech and voice lessons and even started lecturing. She practised for many hours so that she could perform well. She travelled all over the country, addressing audiences. Between her trips she wrote books and articles for various magazines.

At college, her professor had said to her, "God has granted you a priceless gift. You have a unique way of looking at things, and expressing them in a wondrous manner. You must therefore, write your autobiography, for it will inspire many."

Helen Keller wrote her autobiography. People read her book. They marvelled at her confidence and courage. It was indeed, remarkable that a person who could not hear, speak or see was able to reach across to people around the world and inspire them! She started many institutions for the service of the blind.

I look upon Helen Keller as a miracle of our age. She proved to the world that not only could the blind lead the blind, but also the "sighted" – those who could see – by giving them a new vision of life. Aptly she pointed out that if the greedy thought better, the needy would be able to live better. She taught too, that selfishness perverts the mind, while selfless love clears and sharpens one's spiritual vision. To say it in her own beautiful words, "I believe that life is given to us so that we may grow in love, and I believe that God is in me as the sun is in the colour and fragrance of a flower."

Helen Keller was the Messiah of the physically challenged and the differently abled; from her we learn the valuable lesson that disabled people do not need our pity – they would rather have our support and encouragement. She asserted that she scarcely ever stopped to think about her own limitations, and that they never ever made her feel sad – she only felt 'a touch of yearning' at times!

With her great insight and intuition, with her tremendous capacity for learning, her extraordinary determination and strength of spirit, Helen Keller overcame the most adverse of circumstances to lead a full life, and to become a source of support and help to thousands of people across the world. She gave a whole new meaning, indeed, a new dimension to the term we use now – a specially abled person!

Whatever women do they must do twice as well as men to be thought half as good. Luckily, this is not difficult.

- Charlotte Whitton

History, real solemn history, I cannot be interested in.... I read it a little as a duty; but it tells me nothing that does not either vex or weary me. The quarrels of popes and kings, with wars and pestilences on every page; the men all so good for nothing, and hardly any women at all - it is very tiresome.

- Jane Austen
(spoken by Catherine Morland in 'Northanger Abbey')

The history of all times, and of today especially, teaches that ... women will be forgotten if they forget to think about themselves.

- Louise Otto

Chapter 2
Her Story

The Oxford English Dictionary records that it was writer Robin Morgan who coined the term Her Story in her 1970 book, Sisterhood is Powerful.

During the 1970s and 1980s, second-wave feminists saw the study of history as a male-dominated intellectual enterprise and presented "Her Story" as a means of compensation. The term, intended to be both serious and comic, became a rallying cry which even reached the academic world.

In feminist literature and academic discourse, the term has been used as an "economical way" to describe feminist efforts against a male-centered history.

In recent times, a great deal of interest has been evinced in understanding and evaluating the role that women have played in history. This includes not only the study of women's status in society and women's rights throughout recorded history, but also the examination of individual women whose lives and works have had historical significance; and on the other side of the same coin, the effect that historical events have had on women, down the ages. Many scholars have expressed the view that conventional readings of history have tended either to minimise or ignore outright the contributions of women and the effect that historical events had on women as a whole; thus women's history is looked upon as a form of historical 'revisionism', which seeks to challenge or expand the accepted consensus of history.

As recently as March 2010, the US Ambassador to India, Timothy J. Roemer, observed in commemoration of Women's History Month in New Delhi.

(Incidentally, March is observed as Women's History Month in the United States. It highlights contributions of women to events in history and contemporary society.)

India is a remarkable place to celebrate the stature and accomplishments of women. Women have blazed the paths of India's rich history and hold the promise for its bold future. It is no surprise that India boasts a female president, leader of the Congress Party, speaker of Parliament, former Prime Minister, and the first woman to be elected as president of the UN General Assembly. Everyone across the world recognises Nobel Peace Prize winner Mother Teresa, whose work in India has inspired the lives of us all...

Just over a hundred years ago, people insisted that a woman's place was in the home. In the West, women were excluded from voting rights; most colleges and universities would not admit them to higher studies; and all but a few professions were taboo for them. Now women can be found in the halls of Senates and Parliaments, in hospitals, science labs, technology centres, athletic fields and even in outer space. But they didn't arrive there without a struggle!

SAVITRIBAI PHULE

Savitribai Jyotirao Phule was yet another notable social reformer from Maharashtra. Along with her husband, Mahatma Jyotirao Phule, she played a major role in improving women's rights and women's education. She also has the distinction of being the first female teacher of the first women's school in India; as early as 1852, she opened a school for untouchable girls.

Her husband whom we now refer to as Mahatma Jyotirao, was a tremendous source of support and inspiration for Savitribai, as well as her lifelong mentor and guide. It was with his advice and guidance that she was able to take on the cultural mores of a male-dominated society, to take women's education forward. She also made it the mission of her life to tackle the problems of women's rights and the removal of untouchability.

She was involved with Mahatma Phule in every one of his struggles to bring about social reforms. They fought to prevent ill-treatment of widows as well as child-brides; they championed the cause of peasants and workers. Although they faced social ostracization and isolation, they never ever swerved from their cause.

After her husband's demise, Savitribai took over the responsibility of *Satya Shodhak Samaj*, founded by him, presiding over its meetings and guiding its volunteer workers.

She was the first woman to light her husband's pyre in the history of India.

When a plague epidemic struck Maharashtra, Savitribai worked ceaselessly for the victims. She fed nearly two thousand children every day during the epidemic. Tragically, she fell a victim to the dreaded disease when nursing a sick child. She died on March 10, 1897.

Maharashtra remembers this great daughter as *Vidya Jyoti* and *Kranti Jyoti*.

The problem is this, that more often than not, we are so bedazzled by the remarkable and well documented 'achievements' of the modern woman, that we tend to ignore the substantial contributions made by women of earlier ages. Bringing out a special *Guide to Women's History*, the *Encyclopedia Britannica* noted that since the dawn of civilisation, women have left their mark on the world, at times changing the course of history and at other times influencing small but significant spheres of life. But it is only in the past century, that we have begun to make concerted efforts to represent women's contributions more fully in history books. Consequently, the dramatic events that changed the status for many women in modern times, such as the right to own property, to vote and to choose their own careers, may obscure the accomplishments made by women of earlier eras.

We would do well to realise and appreciate that this contribution has been tremendous, though the history books we read in school have failed to record the same.

You will find interspersed in this book, the lives and achievements of some of the great women who have played a magnificent role in shaping the consciousness of women everywhere. It is our way of setting right a lapse that has affected the recorded history of human civilisation.

MADAM CAMA

Bhikhaji Rustom Cama, who is remembered and venerated as one of the most admired figures of India's Independence Movement was born in an affluent Parsi family in Bombay as it was then called, on September 24, 1861. Her parents were Sorabji Framji Patel, a lawyer and a merchant, and Jaijibai Sorabji Patel; they were among the elite of Bombay society in those days.

After receiving her education at the Alexandra Native Girls' English medium School, she married Rustom Cama, a wealthy lawyer, who was a great supporter of the British rulers, and wished to enter politics under their patronage. For Bhikhaji, it was not really a happy marriage, and she spent most of her time and energy in philanthropic activities and social work.

In 1896, the Bombay Presidency was hit by twin disasters – at first, a severe famine, followed by the dreaded bubonic plague. Bhikhaji was a leading member of the many teams working out of Grant Medical College who spared no effort to provide care for the afflicted, and to inoculate the healthy. During this period, she herself contracted plague. Though she managed to survive, she was severely weakened, and her family decided to send her to Britain for medical care and recuperation in 1901.

When she was about to return to India in 1902, she met some of the day's leading Indian nationalists staying in London, and the whole direction of her life changed forever.

The first of them was Shyamji Krishna Varma, who was well known in London's Indian community for his fiery nationalist speeches in Hyde Park. Through him, she met Dadabhai Naoroji, then president of the British Committee of the Indian National Congress. Naoroji was also the first Asian to be elected to the British House of Commons, and she came to work as his private secretary.

Working with Naoroji and Singh Rewabhai Rana, Cama supported the founding of Varma's Indian Home Rule Society in February 1905. Now, the British authorities informed her that she would not be allowed to return to India unless she signed a declaration promising not to participate in nationalist activities. This, she refused to do, remaining in exile in Europe for 34 years, until the last days of her life, returning to Bombay only to breathe her last. But during these years she devoted her considerable fortune and every breath of her life to fight for the cause of her beloved India's freedom.

Now, Madam Cama relocated to Paris, where she co-founded the Paris Indian Society, with other like minded nationalists. In collaboration with members of the movement for Indian sovereignty living in exile, Cama wrote, published and distributed revolutionary literature for the movement, including *Bande Mataram* and *Madan's Talwar* (in response to the execution of Madan Lal Dhingra). These were published in Holland and Switzerland and smuggled into India through the French colony of Pondicherry .

August 22, 1907, was a red letter day for the Nationalists. At the International Socialist Conference in Stuttgart,

Germany, Madam Cama addressed the participants on the devastating effects of a famine that had struck India. She made a strong plea for human rights, equality and freedom from the British yoke and unfurled what she called the Flag of Indian Independence. As she unfurled the flag, she made an impassioned appeal to her audience: "This flag is of Indian Independence! Behold, it is born! It has been made sacred by the blood of young Indians who sacrificed their lives. I call upon you, gentlemen, to rise and salute this flag of Indian Independence. In the name of this flag, I appeal to lovers of freedom all over the world to support this flag."

Co-designed by Cama, Vinayak Damodar Savarkar and Shyamji Krishna Varma, this flag would later serve as one of the templates from which the current national flag of India was created.

In 1909, Madan Lal Dhingra, a revolutionary nationalist living in London, assassinated William Hutt Curzon Wylie, an aide to the Secretary of State for India. The British authorities were incensed; several key activists were arrested in London, among them Vinayak Savarkar. Britain requested France to extradite Madam Cama, but the French authorities refused to do so. In retaliation, Madam Cama's entire inheritance in India was seized by the Crown. It is said that at this point, Lénin actually invited her to come and reside in the Soviet Union; but she declined the invitation.

Madam Cama was influenced by the early leaders of the Suffragette Movement, especially Christabel Pankhurst. Addressing a meeting in Egypt in 1910, she said, "I see here the representatives of only half the population of Egypt. May I ask where is the other half? Sons of Egypt, where are the daughters of Egypt? Where are your mothers and sisters? Your wives and daughters?"

However, it must be stressed that her fight for India's freedom took a precedence over all other efforts. To women who wished to campaign for voting rights in India, she said,

"Let us work for India's freedom and independence. When India is independent women will not only have the right to vote, but all other rights as well."

Her safe exile in Paris was threatened when France became one of Britain's allies during the First world war. She was ordered out of her home in Paris and sought refuge with her friends in Bordeaux. For some time, she was forced to live in Vichy, and could return to Paris only after the war ended in 1918.

Till 1935, she remained in exile, in Europe. When she fell ill and was paralysed by a stroke, she sought permission to return to India. She died in Bombay, at the Parsi General Hospital, on August 13, 1936. Most of her personal assets were bequeathed to a charitable trust.

Today, we remember Madam Cama as the fiery patriot who turned away from a life of affluence and luxury to devote herself to the cause of India's freedom.

Any history that devotes itself exclusively to the lives and deeds of 'great men' must necessarily be the history only of one half of humanity, albeit the 'dominant' half; such history can only be part-history, and not the whole history of the world.

May I add, if the achievements of these women have been left out of the limelight, the record of Indian women who have played a remarkable role in their own era, has suffered from what we now call double discrimination: 1) on account of their being women; 2) on account of their being Indian.

I strongly believe that the world would learn a great deal from the lives of great Indian women starting from our Divine Sita and Radha, through sages like Maitreyi and Gargi, singer-saints like Aandal, Mira and Jana Bai, heroines like Rani Padmini of Chittorgarh and Lakshmibai of Jhansi, to modern legends like Savitribai Phule, Sri Sarada Mani, Kasturba Gandhi and others.

How can we remedy this lapse?

Paul Halsall, who has set up an internet sourcebook for women's history, has multiple solutions to this problem:

The first solution is to locate the great women of the past, following the lead of much popular historiography that focusses on 'great men'. The problem here is that just as the 'great men' approach to history sidelines and ignores the lives of the mass of people, focussing on great women merely replicates the exclusionary historical approaches of the past.

The next solution is to examine and expose the history of oppression of women. This approach had the merit of addressing the life histories of the mass of women, but, since it has proved to be possible to find some degree of oppression everywhere, it tended to make women merely subjects of forces that they could not control. On the other hand, historians' focus on oppression revealed that investigating the structures of women's lives was crucial.

In recent years, while not denying the history of oppression, historians have begun to focus on the agency of women. All human beings are subject to some degree of social forces that limit freedom, but within those limits people are able to exercise greater or lesser degrees of control over their own lives. This insight applies equally to women even in oppressive societies.

Courtesy: Internet Women's History Sourcebook

For Your Reflection...

How much do you know about women's history?

Truth to tell, not a lot!

Try taking this quiz, which may tell you something you didn't know...

1. Which earth goddess and mother of all gods was worshipped at Delphi before the god Apollo began to be worshiped there around 1,000 B.C.?

2. She was blind, deaf and mute from infancy, but went on to become one of the most renowned of lecturers. Can you name her teacher?

3. Who said, "Failure is impossible"?

4. Who was the daughter of Anne Boleyn?

5. Who was the first modern woman to graduate from medical school?

6. About which of these women did a US president reportedly say that her book started a great war?

7. Who said: "Women's history is the primary tool for women's emancipation"?

8. Who was the first woman to be awarded the Nobel Prize for Literature?

9. Who was the Irish woman who regained her faith in God as a result of her exposure to the Indian philosophy of *karma?*

10. What was Florence Nightingale's other area of achievement *apart* from nursing?

Answers:

1. Gaia 2. Ann Sullivan (teacher of Helen Keller) 3. Susan B. Anthony (American Civil Rights leader) 4. Queen Elizabeth I 5. Elizabeth Blackwell M.D. 6. Harriet Beecher Stowe *(Uncle Tom's Cabin)* 7. Gerda Lerner (one of the founders of the field of women's history) 8. Selma Lagerlöf (Swedish writer) 9. Annie Besant 10. Statistics

Culture: mid-15c., "the tilling of land", from L. cultura, from pp. stem of colere "tend, guard, cultivate, till" (see cult). The figurative sense of "cultivation through education" is first attested c.1500. Meaning "the intellectual side of civilisation" is from 1805; that of "collective customs and achievements of a people" is from 1867.

- Online Etymology Dictionary

But the word 'culture' can also mean ritual and tradition and shared values or a way of life. This is the culture that is handed down from generation to generation...Culture is the way humans have passed on their understanding of the world - their world view - to future generations, to understand how things are in the world.

- Robbi Robson
(International Humanist and Ethical Union)

Chapter 3
Custodians Of Culture

For me, the concept of 'culture' is best expressed in Gurudev Sadhu Vaswani's beautiful reflections on the term. In his book, *The Call of Mira Education*, he reminds us:

1. The soul of culture is courtesy. Gentleness is the hallmark of the truly cultured individual.

2. Culture is characterised by humility of spirit. It accepts what Dostevsky described as, "the immeasurable and equal value of every living human soul". Thus the truly cultured person does not push, shout, scold or quarrel.

3. Culture is characterised by understanding; unlike book knowledge, it flows into life and reduces the friction of life.

4. Culture is marked by kindness, sympathy and the spirit of respect shown to everyone, including the disadvantaged and the deprived.

5. Culture is also marked by the spirit of reverence for all life – reverence for what is above us; reverence for what is around us and reverence for what is beneath us.

What a splendid, multi-faceted concept is culture! Little wonder then, that women have been regarded as the preservers, protectors and transmitters of culture in every race and every society! Women's role in culture is central and vital.

Culture is imbibed from childhood, when we listen to our mothers and grandmothers telling us stories from our ancient epics and scriptures. Whoever tells stories, defines culture, is a wise saying indeed! Busy people might argue that today's multi-media world offers many more stories than grandparents and parents can ever hope to narrate; but the trouble, as we all know, is that they represent the wrong culture for our children –

the sort that is known as 'mass' culture, the culture of violence, instant entertainment and mindless fun. Would you really wish to expose your children to that kind of story telling?

Culture is also imbibed from the family environment and the atmosphere of the homes in which we grow up. The deference and reverence that is shown to elders in the family; the habit of receiving visitors courteously, and extending hospitality to them; the experience of shared family meals; the celebration of sacred festivals and family functions; the cherished memory of a mother or grandmother performing the *aarti*, lighting a lamp or saying a prayer... such experiences leave a lasting impression on young minds, sowing the seeds of the cultural heritage that is their birthright.

MA VARAN DEVI
(Mother of Gurudev Sadhu Vaswani)

Gurudev Sadhu Vaswani's mother, Varan Devi, was a pious and devout soul. Though she was not educated, she was a woman of sound sense and practical wisdom. A woman of deep piety, she instilled in her children the habit of reading and memorising passages from the holy scriptures. A great devotee of Guru Nanak, the sacred name *Waheguru* was constantly on her lips and in her heart. She was the spiritual teacher who taught her children to recite from the *Japji Sahib* and the *Sukhmani Sahib*. The children had to recite passages from these scriptures every morning, before breakfast was served to them. It was from her that Sadhu Vaswani imbibed his great reverence for Guru Nanak.

From a very early age, his mother realised that her son was very different from other children of his age. His far away look and his aloofness from shouts and games did not escape her attention. She always tried to reach out to him and soon realised that he was not an ordinary, average child.

She was very young when her husband passed away and the responsibility of bringing up a family of four children devolved upon her. She discharged her duties well and her special love and devotion for her son, Thanwar (Gurudev Sadhu Vaswani), grew with the years. True, she had her own worldly dreams for her son – that he should marry, beget children, take up a lucrative profession and bring honour and glory to the family. It was also true that she distinctly forbade him to even think of uttering the word *fakir* as long as she was alive. In this sense, she held his spiritual aspirations in check as long as she was alive.

But there is another way of looking at this: consider what great affection and reverence Sadhu Vaswani must have had for his mother, if he was ready to set aside his personal aspirations so that she might not be hurt by his choice! Surely, the mother must have meant a lot to this great saint!

His greatest satisfaction as a Professor and Principal must surely have been derived from the fact that his mother came to stay with him in the spacious bungalow allotted to him as his official residence! He never ever left home without touching his mother's feet and seeking her blessings.

When she was on her death bed, Sadhu Vaswani begged her to forgive him for having remained a bachelor despite her earnest entreaties. But she responded with tears in her eyes, "My son, I realise now that you did well in not getting married." She blessed her favourite son and said to him, "You have endeavoured to keep me happy in every way you could. I die a happy woman!"

Family has always played a major role in keeping culture alive and vital, and passing it on to future generations. We in India had, for ages, a prevailing tradition of the joint family system, under which three to four generations, including even extended members of a family like uncles, aunts, cousins, nieces, nephews and their spouses and offspring lived together under one roof. The oldest male member may have been regarded as 'the head of the family' technically; but everyone knew that it was the women who held the family together through the strong bonds of their love, loyalty, integrity and values. A specialist in children's psychology once remarked that children who grew up with their grandparents as part of the family, invariably grew up to be caring, kind and generous. The Indian extended family, nurtured and sustained by its womenfolk, thus fostered good culture and good breeding almost intrinsically.

BHUVANESHWARI DEVI

"Wife and children may desert a man, but his mother never," says Swami Vivekananda. His one unfailing companion and supporter in childhood and boyhood was his own mother, Bhuvaneshwari Devi. His biographers tell us that it was from her that Swamiji inherited not only moral purity and aesthetic sense, but also his phenomenal memory. His mother had a regal bearing and a commanding personality which effortlessly won the respect and veneration of everyone around her. Her illustrious son's influence made the world stand up and take note of him. Undoubtedly, the mother was a great influence on his life.

We are told that as a young boy, Naren as he was called, was restless, spirited and full of pranks and mischief. He also had a quick temper and was prone to angry outbursts. It is said that his mother would press his forehead with cold water, uttering the sacred mantra *Om Namo Shivaya*, to calm his temper tantrums. And she observed with her unfailing sense of humour, "I asked Lord Shiva to send me one of his angels for a son; it looks as if he sent one of his demons instead."

"Never, ever swerve from the path of truth," was a lesson she taught him very early in life. "Even as you will act at all times to protect your dignity, see to it that you do not hurt another's dignity," she taught him.

In 1894, when he was in America, Swami Vivekananda gave a lecture on "The ideals of Indian Women" to the women of Cambridge, in Boston. The women were so impressed by his talk that they wrote a letter to his mother in India. There can be no better tribute to Bhuvaneshwari Devi than this excerpt from the letter:

"...we, who have your son in our midst, send you greetings. His generous service to men, women and children in our midst was laid at your feet by him in an address he gave us the other day on 'The Ideals of Indian Women'. The worship of his mother will be to all who heard him an inspiration and an uplift... Accept, dear Madam, our grateful recognition of your life and work in and through your son. And may it be accepted by you as a slight token of remembrance to serve in its use as a tangible reminder that the world is coming to its true inheritance from God, Brotherhood and Unity."

Religion, language, attitudes, beliefs, customs, traditions, festivals, art and even food and cuisine are aspects, indeed components of culture. I cannot stress adequately, the importance that we must give to strengthening and empowering our cultural traditions in this age of technology and globalisation, when the focus is on trade, commerce, business and material acquisition. When diasporic communities, like my own native Sindhi community, lose touch with their religious beliefs, their mother tongue and their community traditions, they are actually destroying their own precious cultural heritage!

For Your Reflection

Tory MP, Richard Graham, has come under fire for saying that women are putting themselves at risk of rape by wearing short skirts and high heels.

Graham's comments sparked outrage among women's groups, who insist that if a woman becomes a victim of rape it is not because of her dress style.

Vivienne Hayes, of the Women's Resource Centre said such comments frighteningly normalise victim-blaming. They reallocate blame from the perpetrator to the victim. The problem is not female vulnerability but a macho culture, which produces the notion of male entitlement – a culture which consistently fails women through disbelief, victim-blaming and failure to investigate, she added.

– Courtesy: *Daily Mail*

The inspiring force of the home is the woman. The home is the origin and beginning of every form of social organisation. It is the nursery of the nation. It is the sweet place wherein children are trained for future citizenship. The woman illumines the home through the glory of motherhood. Man is incapable of doing those duties incident upon the rearing of children. Good habits, right conduct and formation of good character are created in children spontaneously in a well regulated home under the personal influence of the mother. The loving kindness and the cultured gentleness of the mother help the children to unfold their native talents and dormant capacities quickly. Children absorb ideas by suggestion and imitation. Early training and impressions formed at an early age are lasting. The mother at home can do the formation of character very efficiently. Therefore, home is the most beautiful training ground for the building of character in children under the personal guidance of the mother.

If the mother trains her children on the right lines from an early age, she is rendering great service indeed to the nation and national culture. Women have good and ample opportunities of improving national health and increasing prosperity. It is they who really build the nation. They can utilise their talents and abilities in making the home a cradle of culture, character, personal ability and religious revival.

– **Swami Sivananda**

Marriage is the only institution that allows two people to establish a very strong and enduring relationship that is fully backed by the law and society as a whole. This is the main reason why the institution of marriage has been around for so long.

No other emotional and social bond comes close to this institution in its depth and scope.

- James Walsh

I enter this house with a happy heart. May I give birth to children, who observe the path of righteousness (dharma)! May this house that I enter today be prosperous forever and never be deficient in food. May this house be populated by people of virtue and pious thoughts.

- Vedic mantra uttered by the wife as she enters her marital abode

Chapter 4

Marriage: Two Halves, One Whole

Top Ten reasons to get married:

10. Marriage makes you live longer

9. Marriage increases your earning power

8. Marriage is the starting point of every family

7. Marriage prevents you from dying alone

6. Marriage makes you more acceptable and attractive, socially

5. Marriage brings financial benefits

4. Marriage means happier and more fulfilling relationships

3. Marriage means stability and security

2. Married people are happier

1. Marriage makes you a better person

Top Ten reasons NOT to get married:

10. The spouse always alters – for the worse

9. Marriage is the end of your freedom

8. Marriage is expensive

7. Marriage just makes for a lot of paperwork

6. Marriage is the end of spontaneity

5. Marriage is constant compromise

4. Marriage puts an end to your best friendships

3. Marriage often fails

2. Marriage puts an end to your sense of adventure and risk

1. Marriage ties you down for life

– **Results of a survey in the US.**

Someone remarked to me once that most books on marriage and most advice on making a marriage work are largely addressed to women rather than men. That is not surprising, because we assume that women have the ability, the emotional intelligence and the power to make a marriage work!

Let me make it very clear at the outset: when I say that women can make a marriage work, I do not mean that they are the ones who must bend and bow and submit to the men. I only mean that a woman has those special qualities that can make for a win-win relationship. In any case, this book is not about marriage, but about women!

Utter submission and subordination from any one partner can never make for a happy marriage – and this is true now, as it was in the past. I doubt if any man can be happy and satisfied in a marriage in which his wife is withdrawn and unhappy – a passive victim. I am convinced that if someone were to make a well-researched study of the institution of marriage, we are likely to find that over the millennia, over the centuries, a good marriage has become happier, more equitable, fairer, more fulfilling and better at fostering the well-being of adults and children in the family.

Some of you might turn around and ask me: How then do we account for the increase in divorces and breaking marriages?

My answer would simply be this: in view of changing expectations and changing social mores, men and women have to work harder, give more commitment and dedication, and become more understanding and empathetic to keep the spark in their marriages! There are no special rules, no magic formulae, no instant 'intervention' that can substitute this kind of hard work and solid, dependable qualities. To answer the question directly, divorces are increasing because men and women are not working hard enough to make a success of their marriage; they are not committed enough.

Till the early decades of the twentieth century advice to women on marriage and family came largely from mother figures, older women or from religious authorities, priests and scriptural references. In more recent times, psychologists, sociologists and marriage counselors have taken on that role.

As one expert remarks, "The role of marriage in society and personal life has changed more in the past 30 years than in the previous 3,000, primarily because of the new opportunities for women to live independent lives. In consequence, everything we used to think we knew about how marriage works – and why it doesn't work – is changing."

When a friend showed me the results of the survey that I have shared with you, it occurred to me that this was largely representative of the views of men. I enquired of my friend whether there was an opinion poll directed more specifically at women – and that too, a broad spectrum of women.

He came back with a few key findings which I share with you:

- The role of women in the urban societies has been changing radically over the past four decades brought about largely by changes in their economic and social status.

- Many women in the US are less likely to marry than ever before, according to the findings of Rutgers University National Marriage Project (1999).

- Marriage is no longer the top priority for a number of young women. This is largely attributed to the many options that today's women have before them. Marriage is not the only road to happiness for women.

- Many research studies reveal that women are increasingly placing more value on their independence and autonomy which they feel will help them achieve their personal goals.

- Many women believe that it is men who actually benefit more from marriage, according to numerous statistics – in terms of better health, better income, etc.

- The male breadwinner or female homemaker model may no longer be the desired norm for happy union.

- The changing roles in marriage (i.e. house-husband and working wife or the wife as the leading provider) are not always deliberately chosen or planned by the couple; more often they happen as a reaction to unexpected financial pressures.

Sociologists say that financially independent women can be more selective in choosing their marriage partners and they also have more 'negotiating power' within the marriage.

What all these bewildering 'findings' and 'statistics' reveal is that while attitudes to marriage are changing, perhaps the so-called gender stereotypes and gender roles themselves are changing. And these changes bring their own new set of challenges with them.

"I do not need to marry for a meal ticket," a young woman said to me confidently. "I'm looking for respect and equality in marriage."

While I was happy that the young lady doesn't have to "marry for money" as they used to put it in those days, the thought did cross my mind that many men might find those new expectations difficult to meet. Men too have to struggle with age-old expectations that they must be the principal breadwinners. They too must get used to the idea that they have to share the housework and child-rearing along with their wives. They associate their identity with being providers and breadwinners; they see their value as bringing in money. If their spouses want them to be empathetic, egalitarian and share the housework, how much joy and pride and enthusiasm can they bring into these tasks and into marriage as a whole?

There are two broad views of marriage in circulation among lay people today. We draw our understanding of marriage from both these views.

The first view holds that Marriage is an essentially private, intimate, emotional relationship created by two people for their own personal reasons to enhance their own personal well-being. Marriage is created by the couple, for the couple.

The second view of Marriage is that it is essentially a social contract between two individuals who wish to unite their lives legally, economically and socially.

Most religious faiths regard marriage as a sacrament which binds a man and woman in the union of holy wedlock for a lifetime. Thus, a Hindu marriage is performed before a *havan* fire, amidst *vedic* chants, with *agni deva* as witness; a Christian wedding is usually solemnised in a Church and a Sikh wedding is performed in a *Gurudwara*, amidst the chanting of prayers. In each of these, a priest or appointed religious authority officiates in the ceremony.

All over the world today, we continue to have love marriages as well as arranged marriages. Love may begin with physical attraction but marriage, in due course, fuses the couple together so that they form one complete whole. This is the purpose of marriage. When we forget it, we lose the proper perspective of marriage.

One of the most unfortunate 'developments' in the modern age is that the all-pervasive spirit of competition has managed to enter even the sacred sphere of marriage. I do not wish to say much about men's or women's liberation, but it is tragic if such ideologies are allowed to divide marriages.

Men and women were made to be different. God, in His wisdom, meant them to complement each other. I am aware that many liberalists today will take umbrage over that statement, because they disagree on the basic concept that there is a difference! Let me state categorically: I do *not* subscribe to the theory of women as "the weaker sex". They are not weaker – they are different, that's all! The husband's and wife's roles in marriage are *different* – and one cannot be played by the other, no matter what young men and women think today. A woman is strong in qualities of the heart – intuition, sensibility and sympathy. The man is strong in qualities of the head. They should blend their 'selves' together so that the union is wholesome and meaningful. Most importantly for a marriage, women are born nurturers; it is their unique trait that they can love and share and care as a man perhaps cannot.

Many experts say that men are biologically programmed to be providers, protectors and fixers, in short, what we refer to as "a man about the house". So too, biologically, women are nurturers. Care-giving comes naturally to them. But this does not mean that they should go unappreciated or taken for granted.

If these experts are to be believed, many women do not care about the stereotyped role of nurturer and caregiver – patient, long-suffering, sacrificing for the sake of family. But many women do value what they call the softer side of their nature, their special skills in building and maintaining personal relationships.

Today, many women are struggling to forge their own identity, build a career, trying to stand on their own feet and improving their financial position, in a world that is still a male bastion. Some of them are actually beginning to ask whether they should reject the traditional notions of woman as nurturer and caregiver.

Rebecca Kourlis, a lady who has served as a US State Supreme Court Justice since 1995, thinks that this will not work: "Perhaps we have come far enough in our progression toward personal and professional equality to recognise and honour those traits that historically represented the feminine in society," she writes. "We need those traits as people, to be whole."

One of the most famous mothers of the last century – Mother Teresa – offered this advice to women:

> Spread love everywhere you go, first of all in your own house. Give love to your children, to your husband, to the next door neighbour … Let no one ever come to you without leaving better and happier. Be the living expression of God's kindness; kindness in your face, kindness in your eyes, kindness in your smile, kindness in your warm greeting.

Women are strong in spiritual *shakti*. Biologically too, they can tolerate more pain. They are much better at handling stress. Fewer women die of heart-attacks. They take on suffering and adversity in ways that men cannot. That is why they have been described as "shock absorbers".

Yes, in many ways women are spiritually and emotionally stronger than men. This is why I think that it is up to the woman to establish, strengthen and nurture the institution of marriage. Let me reiterate: to marry or not to marry is an individual's choice; but once a couple enters the state of marriage, both of them have to work hard to make the marriage successful!

Women have been exploited and discriminated against. This has led to a sense of insecurity and anger. This has led to some women actually questioning the very basis of marriage, as they feel that it is a social institution that is only meant to enslave them and exploit them.

We should learn to respect women – respect, revere and love them. But it is my appeal to all my sisters, that as women, they too, should accept their responsibility as creators of the home, as mothers, as guardians and custodians of the sacred institution of marriage. This requires that they attain inner harmony and serenity. Then will our homes be centres of peace, joy and love!

Many young women ask me if they can exercise the right to remain single; my answer is that they have every right to choose their life state.

Though I hold both marriage and motherhood to be sacred, I would be the last one to insist that they should be imposed on any one. I know several sisters who have had the inner urge to dedicate their lives to a cause greater than themselves. Exceptions to the rule must be permitted graciously and leniently. Gurudev Sadhu Vaswani once remarked that a woman could exercise far greater influence as a mother than as a missionary; but some women are born to be missionaries – to dedicate themselves to a cause that they hold dear.

Divorce rates are soaring among India's newly affluent middle classes, as working women with independent incomes refuse to submit to the traditional ideal of marriage. Cases in New Delhi have doubled in five years to a projected figure of 8,000 for 2005, with similar rises seen in Kolkata, Mumbai and Bangalore.

Most marriages in India are still arranged by the parents, with the bride and groom meeting on only two or three occasions before the ceremony. The bride is expected to move into her husband's house where – for the first four or five years at least – the couple get to know each other under the guidance of their joint or extended family.

But a new breed of independently-minded women is often not well-adapted to this role. The virtues of individualism and self-reliance that are prized by employers who are vying for the services of bright young graduates do not sit easily with the accepted role of a Hindu wife.

In Bangalore, India's showcase tech-city, where women work in call centres and as IT managers, the number of divorces tripled between 1988 and 2002.

Opinion is divided over what the phenomenon means: for traditionalists the rising numbers portend the breakdown of society while some modernists speak of a healthy new empowerment for women.

– The Daily Telegraph (2005)

MAITREYI

In the Upanishads, a beautiful story is told to us, about Rishi Yagnavalkya and his wife Maitreyi. Maitreyi was a remarkable woman – one in a million.

Rishi Yagnavalkya actually had two wives, Katyayani and Maitreyi. Maitreyi was one of the most distinguished and pre-eminently wise women of ancient India. Athirst with keen aspiration to gain knowledge of the Vedas and Upanishads and the sacred *Shastras*, she became the wife of Rishi Yagnavalkya.

Although she performed her duties as a *rishi patni* with meticulous care and devotion, Maitreyi was constantly in quest of supreme knowledge that would transcend the material life of this world. Above all, she longed to be a *shishya,* a true disciple to her husband.

Rishi Yagnavalkya, who was then engaged in compiling and codifying his *Yagnavalkya Smriti* (on Jurisprudence and Law), decided to seek *sanyasa*. In those days, it was the custom of the *rishis* and sages, that after a certain period in *grihasta ashrama*, they would retire to the *tapobana*, or forest of meditation, to seek the Highest Truth, unhampered, unfettered by worldly cares and concerns. But this had to be done with due care and concern for the welfare of their wives, whom they would be leaving behind.

He explained his decision to his two wives, Katyayani and Maitreyi. "Dear ones, my spiritual aspirations incline me to take up *sanyasa*, the life of renunciation. I am concerned about your well-being, as I shall have to leave both of you behind. But here is a good amount of gold that will enable you to live in comfort. Give me leave to take up the quest that my soul desires."

Katyayani, a simple, obedient and devout woman,

accepted her husband's instructions without protest. But Maitreyi could not be put off so easily.

The wise woman that she was, Maitreyi said to her husband, "*Swami,* you are leaving behind you a great deal of gold, which is very valuable. And you say you go in search of something else that your heart desires. Am I right in assuming then, that what you seek is far more valuable than gold? Would you please tell me what is this precious thing that you seek, which all this gold cannot buy?"

"My quest is for Liberation, to attain the Lotus Feet of the Lord, beyond the heaven world," replied Rishi Yagnavalkya. "It is a state that transcends grief and death. No amount of gold can buy this for me. Now that you know what I seek, will you let me go?"

"Will the gold that you are leaving with me enable me to attain Liberation?"

"No, my dear, it will not," said the sage. "Liberation cannot be attained through wealth."

"In that case," said Maitreyi humbly, "of what use is the settlement which cannot lead me to the goal I seek? Therefore, tell me how I may attain what I seek."

Rishi Yagnavalkya was very pleased with this earnest request. In his unsurpassed spiritual wisdom, he realised her earnest aspiration, and revealed to her the supreme knowledge of the *Atman.*

The immortal dialogue between Rishi Yagnavalkya and Maitreyi is recorded in the *Brihadaranyaka Upanishad.*

Thus, did Maitreyi attain the supreme knowledge of self-realisation.

The angel of the Family is Woman. Mother, wife or sister; woman is the caress of life, the soothing sweetness of affection shed over its toils, a reflection of the individual of the loving providence which watches over humanity. In her there is a treasure enough of consoling tenderness to allay every pain. Moreover for every one of us she is the initiator of the future. The mother's first kiss teaches the child love; the first holy kiss of the woman he loves teaches man hope and faith in life; love and faith create a desire for perfection and the power of reaching towards it step by step; create the future, in short, of which the living symbol is the child, link between us and the generations to come. Through her the Family, with its Divine mystery of reproduction, points to Eternity.

-Giuseppe Mazzini

A family can develop only with a loving woman as its center.

- Friedrich Schlegel

Chapter 5
Family: The Heart Of The Matter

Hindu families demonstrate firm ties of affection, strikingly different from many western families. Hindu scriptures have elaborately defined the dynamics of the various relationships within families. For example, a grandchild can tease and joke with a grandparent in a familiar way, not permissible with the father or mother. The different relatives are given specific terms of address, unlike the West where "aunt" or "uncle" refers to a whole host of relatives and family friends.

The extended family traditionally provides shelter and support for the elderly, the disabled and the less well off. Children are expected to repay the debt owed to their parents by supporting them in their retirement and old age. An important aspect of Hindu family life is the inter-dependence between members. Marriage itself is a broad social and religious obligation, rather than just a relationship between partners. The extended family provides considerable practical and emotional support, as for example when children are born. One advantage is that marriage stability is not inordinately reliant on the state of the couple's emotional ties. Despite these possible benefits, social trends indicate that the extended family is becoming less popular, especially outside India. Young couples often value the freedom that the nuclear family offers. They are also adopting other aspects of the Western lifestyle. TV is becoming more popular than worship and is certainly influencing family values strongly.

– The Heart of Hinduism

The Webster Dictionary offers us multiple definitions of the world 'family' starting with a basic one: "all the people living in the same house"; later definitions are more inclusive: "a group of people related by ancestry or marriage" and "all those claiming descent from a common ancestor; tribe or clan; lineage".

The Arab term for family is *aila*. The root meaning of that word is "to support".

The Chinese word for "nation", we are told, consists of the combination of two other characters: *"guo"* – country – and *"jia"* – family. That is, a nation or a people of one nationality, are families living in the same country. In other words, the family is accorded the status of the basic unit of a nation or a society.

The American writer, George Santayana, described the family as "one of nature's masterpieces".

In our survey of 'family' definitions, we have moved from the purely technical and legal, through the sociological and emotional to the purely idealistic! Here is one more – a sarcastic definition, whose source I have not been able to trace: "Families mean support and an audience to men. To women, they just mean more work".

I must say I cannot help sympathising with the gist of that remark – that the onus of responsibility of the family (as for so much else in life) rests with the true heroines of this world and this book – the women!

I have made no secret of my firm belief that the twentieth century was the era that spelt out in clear terms, the freedom of women. Education, career, family and marriage – all of these are options open to women everywhere today; and we would do well to remember that it was not the case earlier! But still, many women feel that they have not been fairly treated in the workplace or in the family.

JIJABAI

Jijabai was the mother of Chhatrapati Shivaji Maharaj, who is the greatest hero of Maharashtra.

Jijau, as she was called, was born to Mhalsabai and Lakhoji Jadhav, a commanding officer in charge of the Sindakhed territory under Mughal rule. Thus she was exposed to a military environment from birth. At an age when other young girls were playing with their dolls and their pots and pans to prepare themselves for a married life, Jijau was learning the fine art of sword fighting. Her mother Mhalsai nurtured Jijau's courage by narrating great tales of valour to the girl. Excited and inspired by these tales, Jijau begged her father to send her for armament training.

Even at that young age, Jijau was saddened by the plight of the Hindus under alien rule. She was ashamed of some of the men she saw around her – men who could do nothing to protect their women, children, culture, country and religion.

Jijau was married to Shahaji Raje Bhosale in 1605. Although he was an accomplished warrior, he was essentially undervalued by his Mughal masters. She realised that she and her family were in servitude under the Muslim rulers, with no recognition, security or benefit of the community.

She finally found recourse in prayer by appealing to Bhavani, the Goddess of valour and the deity of this land. She entreated the Goddess to give her a son who would be bright, accomplished and immensely capable of establishing *Swarajya*. The mighty Goddess heard her faithful devotee's prayer and Jijabai was soon blessed with the birth of Shivaji.

Chhatrapati Shivaji was extremely devoted to his mother Jijabai, who was deeply religious. She was educated, able and wielded great authority; her historical personality belies the myth of the "oppressed Hindu woman of medieval India". She was responsible for most of Chhatrapati Shivaji's education.

She was determined to make her son the new leader of a new generation who could take on these responsibilities. She carefully studied the complex political problems of her day, and infused a love of liberty in her infant son. She taught him values and lessons from the *Mahabharata* and the *Ramayana*. He was also sent to learn about the holy scriptures and arts of administration and weaponry, and the political situations in the land. To this day, her memory is honoured as the great mother of a great emperor. Her life story is a testimonial to *narishakti*! A mother is the shaper of her child's destiny and collectively, mothers have the power to shape the destiny of an entire nation! Mothers alone can sow the seeds of high values in the young impressionable minds of children. The health and well being of a society, indeed the progress and prosperity of a nation, depends on these values.

Chhatrapati Shivaji was a great military leader, a hero in his lifetime. He had built the powerful Maratha empire almost single handedly. But he was endowed with special qualities of head and heart which made him a great human being! And these special qualities, he imbibed from his caring mother! He was a true *Guru bhakta:* he symbolically offered the keys of his kingdom, and his royal scepter at the feet of his Guru, Samarth Ramdas. He said to his Guru, "I surrender my entire kingdom to you. Please accept it. From today onwards I wish to be an ordinary citizen. I want to live like a common man. This kingdom now belongs to you." Imagine the humility of that great warrior king! He willingly accepted the post of a 'custodian'. He ruled his kingdom according to the teachings of his Guru.

Chhatrapati Shivaji was truly a noble man. In his impeccable, spotless character and courage, his mother Jijabai's contribution is enormous. Today, she is credited with raising Shivaji in a manner that led to his future greatness. She is regarded as an ideal mother. Her upbringing of Shivaji is the subject of folklore and legend all over India.

I repeat this because it is worth repeating: Woman is the centre of the home and hence, she is the integrating force of society. Needless to say, the mother's role is vital in making the home heaven-like. It is her nature, her qualities, her temperament which will go to build her home and influence her children. It is her personality which is stamped upon the home she lives in – and the family she raises.

It has always been the traditional role of the women in the family to stay at home and manage the domestic sphere while the male members of the family went out to work. The second half of the twentieth century was a period that challenged this idea. With unforeseen, indeed unprecedented economic opportunities opening up along with their attendant social pressures, women and men today are engaged in a struggle to balance the often competing demands of work and family life.

Prof. Jonathon Gershuny, a sociologist, has labelled a late twentieth syndrome among professional couples which he calls Allerednic – which, as you can make out, is Cinderella spelt backwards; it is the syndrome of the fairy tale in reverse. An equal princess marries her handsome prince and he turns her into his scullery maid! In other words, the world may have changed, social norms may have changed, but the 'double burden' is still the woman's cross to bear.

Having grown up in the benign shadow of a saint who believed in the power of the woman-soul, having been a witness and a participant in a great educational movement named after a woman saint and aimed at the upliftment of women, I have indeed rejoiced to see many women rise to positions of distinction, taking their rightful place in an increasingly professionalised world of work and business. But the anxiety persists with many members of my generation that the rapid changes we see around us today are beginning to undermine the very spirit of family values and indeed, the essential character of the family as we know it. What would truly grieve me is to find that the empowerment and upliftment of women, their justified economic, legal and social rights are, in some way, also contributing to the slow dissolution of marriage and family, and this, at an exorbitantly high cost to children and old people. It is not just a broad generalisation that I am making. And I want to illustrate this by what follows.

In some western countries, and in India in recent times, it is now taken to be the fundamental right of a woman to have access to abortion-on-demand. 'Legal' abortion was justified on the grounds that working women needed to be given the right *not* to have children, or to have children only when they choose, in order to facilitate their careers. Of course, we refer to this legal killing by a flowery term, a euphemism: medical termination of pregnancy.

Consider how ironic this is, when many women are fighting for their right to have children, through adoption and through highly sophisticated fertility treatments! Consider the medico-legal complications of surrogate children and the rights of their biological and adoptive parents. And add to this, the complexities that arise when the child and its adoptive parents do not share the same racial, religious or cultural background.

Today, single parenthood, divorce and unmarried motherhood are all contributing to gradual demise of the two-parent family, which was perceived as the very basis of civilised society. Despite our 'sophistication' and 'progress' we cannot take away the trauma of a divided family, with children having to grow up without the care and the support of one of their parents. And we are witnessing today the unseemly wrangling between fathers who are not willing to pay for the upkeep of their own children and mothers refusing to take responsibility for their offspring.

It is my humble opinion that when parental responsibilities have to be enforced by law, a human being's highest values and feelings are trampled in the dust!

At the other end of the spectrum is the equally horrific prospect of old people being neglected, ill-treated, sometimes abused, harassed, physically and mentally tortured and even driven out of their homes by unnatural sons and daughters. Newspapers report that more than 50% of all the cases of elderly abuse, which in some cases is both physical and verbal, are by adult children who want to grab land or houses owned by their aged parents.

Chennai is one of the most traditional and culture-conscious metros in India. A 2012 survey by Help Age India among senior citizens in Chennai showed that close to 28% of elderly people in the city suffer abuse. Disrespect – (44%) and neglect – (30%) were reported to be the most common form of abuse. A larger survey taken up in 2011, however, also showed an alarming increase in physical abuse of the elderly. While only 8.4% of the elderly in Chennai reported physical abuse in 2010, nearly 39% reported physical abuse in 2011, a four-fold increase.

A few years ago, the Chennai High Court invoked the law to enforce a son to take care of his old parents, who had been disowned by him – after he had collected their pensions, provident fund, and had the ancestral house made over in his name! Is it not a shame that we need laws to remind us of our family obligations?

Shakespeare's King Lear dramatises the tragedy of a king, an old man, father of three grown-up daughters, who decides to divide his kingdom among them so that he may live the autumn of his life free from cares and worldly responsibilities. Unfortunately, he disinherits one of them, his favourite daughter, because she refuses to flatter his ego by telling him how much she loves him. His kingdom is given to the two other elder daughters. No sooner do they inherit his power and his wealth, than they begin to reveal their true colours. The old father is insulted, abused and finally turned out of doors on a stormy night to brave the elements. Unable to comprehend, leave alone come to terms with such blatant ingratitude, the old king loses his sanity.

What would you say – a familiar story these days?

Contrast this with the story of our own Pundalik, saint of Maharashtra. He was a great Krishna *bhakta,* who was also devoted to the service of his aged parents. Legends tell us that one day, Lord Krishna and his wife Rukmini came to visit his *bhakta* and called out to him, announcing their arrival outside his humble cottage. Pundalik was, at that time, engaged in massaging the aching feet of his old parents. On hearing the Lord call out his name, Pundalik threw a couple of bricks out through the door of the cottage, and asked Sri Krishna and his consort to stand on the bricks and wait a while, until he attended to his parents. The concession of the bricks was made to the Lord because the outside of the cottage was sticky and slushy with mud, and the Lord could at least keep his sacred feet dry while he waited outside. The Lord for His part, stood patiently on the *vit* (brick) thus becoming Vitthala to generations of *bhaktas* subsequently!

How are our old parents faring today?

"Every old man is also a King Lear," said Goethe, the German writer. Indeed, old age homes in twenty-first century India, are full of old men and women who have not only given the best years of their life to their children – but also bestowed their life-savings, pensions and provident fund on their offsprings in the fond hope that they will be loved and cared for in their old age – only to be 'dumped' in such homes when the children no longer need them!

I do not exaggerate. A distinguished social worker from Chennai, who has dedicated her life to caring for such destitute senior citizens, remarked that old mothers and fathers are literally driven out of their homes when they are no longer 'useful' – when the mother is too old to cook and clean and take care of the house, and the father is too ill or senile to fetch rations and pay utility bills and walk the children to school and back.

That is not all. She also says that when these 'orphaned' old people die in the old age homes, their sons and daughters do not bother to arrange for their last rites, or even attend the funerals arranged by the volunteers serving in the homes. Some of them send a little money to cover funeral expenses. Others simply express their inability to attend the funeral and tell the volunteers to do whatever they think fit!

No, this is not fiction. It is reality. In a particular lawsuit filed by destitute parents, the court has actually ordered the sons to look after their parents or pay a certain amount to them for their upkeep.

The fundamental values of our society are being eroded with the fragmentation of families and the rejection of old people. What are we going to do about it?

Across the oceans and continents, in the Pacific island paradise of Haiti, which was recently devastated by an earthquake, a Red Cross report indicates that it is the island's women, many of them either unemployed or earning low wages who are playing a vital role in the rehabilitation of the nation. In Haiti, the rights of women remain weak, and as such, in the chaos of the aftermath of the earthquake their protection from violence was often overlooked. Displacement, loss of shelter, lack of security provisions by government, crowded living conditions and poorer access to medical facilities and economic opportunities have threatened their lives and livelihoods.

But yet, the report says, it is these women who have held the society together. Many of them now find themselves with larger families, as they take in children and elderly relatives, despite shrinking or non-existent incomes.

There is ample evidence that, given modest opportunity and support, women are extremely efficient providers for their families, insulating against the threats of poverty and hunger. Several well-known economic studies have found that women are more likely than men to spend extra income on the health and education of the children, thereby reducing the inter-generational transmission of poverty. A research study on pensioners in South Africa also reported that children living in the homes of female pensioners with increased pension benefits had higher anthropometric (height for age and weight for height) scores than did children living in the households of comparable male pensioners. Mothers or grandmothers, wives or sisters, women have always been more caring, more selfless, more concerned about the welfare of their families!

Truly, it has been said that the home is the door to the Kingdom of God, the kingdom of true happiness. But you cannot just buy or rent a heaven-like home readymade and offered to you for the asking! It is the women of the family who can turn a brick-and-mortar house or dwelling into a *home* where love, joy, peace, commitment, values and mutual understanding flourish.

Needless to say, the mother's role is vital in making the home heaven-like. It is her nature, her qualities, her temperament which will go to build her home and influence her children. It is her personality which is stamped upon the home she lives in and the family she raises. And the mother is also the wife of the householder; the daughter-in-law to her husband's parents; the sister-in-law to his siblings; in short, the *Griha lakshmi*, as she is referred to in India.

"*Griha lakshmi!* That name makes me see red!" a young lady once remarked. "They bestow the title of a goddess upon us and treat us worse than slaves. I reject both the pedestal and the job profile of a *griha lakshmi*. I have no wish whatsoever to be a goddess. I am human, and I demand my fundamental human rights! I want freedom to do as I please."

I would like to ask all my sisters: What price are we prepared to pay for our freedom? Can you evade your duties and responsibilities and sacred obligations in the name of freedom? What social costs are you ready to pay (and make others pay) for the sake of your freedom?

The ancient law giver Manu, is a much maligned figure for many people today. It was he who said: "Where women are honoured there reside the Gods." Wives were referred to as *ardhangini* (an equal half) or *sahadharmini* (one who participated with equal right, in upholding *Dharma*). Therefore, as I explained earlier, the sanctified union of marriage symbolises the coming together of two complementary and equal halves, to form one beautiful whole.

A scholar of our ancient texts puts it thus: "Man married mainly to sustain *dharma*, with his wife as an equal partner. He had his part to play and she had hers. Nothing was considered inferior and nothing was considered superior. Duty, responsibility and obligation formed the core of one's life. The Vedic seers were firmly of the view that it was only when these virtues were given primacy, that there would be harmony in society and human life could be sustained properly. Today, most virtues are summarily dismissed on one of two counts. Either one says it is irrelevant or one says it is not workable in this day and age. I believe both arguments are false and escapist."

A recent research project carried out in America concludes: "Motherhood remains a career liability for women, while fatherhood is actually a career asset. Women are still doing most of the child care, while men with stable family lives advance faster than single men. Families seem to be more stable when mothers work long hours than when fathers do."

This is true in East and West. Mothers and wives have traditionally taken the greatest responsibility for family life.

Married women will say that this is a one-sided argument to illustrate the point that women are responsible for the well-being of the family and I agree with them; it is equally up to the men, to help their wives make the home a happy, harmonious haven for the children to grow up.

The family state in our ancient Sanskrit language is referred to as *grihasta ashrama*. Mark this: The family, the home or household, is considered as an *ashrama* – a place of discipline; *not* a pleasure hunting ground. Marriage is not a license. It is at once a discipline and a responsibility.

In a happy and successful family, a husband and wife should love and respect each other, and seek to bring out the best in each other. They should help each other to grow in the spirit of love, understanding, forgiveness and selflessness. They should support each other to evolve and unfold their highest potential. If this is kept in focus as the goal of marriage, love and harmony will prevail in the home.

Here is a beautiful prayer that I came across in a book:

Let there be harmony between husband and wife.
Let there be harmony between parents and their children.
Let there be harmony among different relatives.
Let there be harmony among friends.
Let there be harmony among the elements.
Let there be harmony between the earth and the sky.
Let harmony be experienced everywhere!
May God bless you with harmony and peace!

Above all, parents must realise that children are not their 'toys' or 'personal achievements'; nor are they the future insurance for their parents. They are souls whom God has entrusted to your care. You are not expected to pamper or indulge them mindlessly; rather, you must blend firmness with affection, discipline with love; to give them a secure and healthy environment where they might grow to absorb the deeper values of life.

Humility and understanding are the keys to harmony and happiness in the home. When family members learn to love and appreciate each other and their children, then familial bonds are strengthened.

To understand is to stand under! Therefore, understanding helps you to grow in the spirit of humility. Unfortunately humility is becoming a rare virtue these days. Nobody wants to stand *under* anyone – everyone wants to stand above everyone else – no wonder then, that the divorce rate is increasing and homes are breaking! Parents say they cannot understand their children; children claim that they cannot understand their parents.

"Why should we stay at home and look after the children?" young women argue. "Let our husbands do the cooking, cleaning and child-minding!"

"Why on earth should I help with the children and the house work?" husbands want to know. "I bring in the money, and I will not lift a finger in my own home!"

Many youngsters today, especially in urban settings, have grown up as children of working mothers, and have known the pros and cons of being in a situation where their parents have not always been there for them. Some of their parents have been work-centric, rather than family-centric. (i.e. placing more emphasis on their careers than on their families). In fact, if recent research is to be believed, members of the new generation are becoming more family-centric than their parents.

Both men and women must fulfill their role in sustaining and nourishing family values. This calls for a little more empathy among marriage partners. Empathy is nothing but understanding the other person's point of view. The golden command, "do-as-you-would-be-done-by", is a splendid instance of empathy. It is an excellent technique for strengthening marriage bonds and making the home a happy haven.

I urge young people to enter into marriage and family life with a serious sense of commitment, integrating head and heart. It is a commitment one makes for a lifetime and not to be taken lightly. When you enter marriage with this sense of commitment, your home is sure to become a temple of love, peace, joy and harmony – a centre of light amidst the encircling darkness. The love and peace that emanates from such homes reaches out and radiates towards others. The parents and children from these homes have the wonderful ability to love and serve others, and can become the catalysts who transform society.

For Your Reflection

The recent Atlantic magazine cover article, "Why Women Still Can't Have It All?" is making waves amongst women, feminists and professionals by asking the ever-controversial question: "Can women have it all?"

The article, written by Anne-Marie Slaughter, an international affairs professor at Princeton, former director of policy planning at the US State Department, and former dean of Princeton's Woodrow Wilson School of Public and International Affairs, discusses her experience as a professional woman who constantly felt pulled in two different directions trying to achieve the ever-elusive "work-life balance".

A mother of two sons, Slaughter ultimately made the decision that having only weekends at home with her family was not enough, and left her post at the State Department in Washington, D.C., to return full-time to Trenton, N.J., where her family lives.

After detailing her experience, she lays out several ways in which American culture must change in order to make "having it all" a possibility for professional mothers. She discusses how the culture of work time – staying late at the office, working weekends – must be adapted to accommodate working parents (mothers and fathers) so they can work from home when necessary. Workplaces must also consider time spent with children or fulfilling family obligations with equal respect as time spent on other outside activities – like marathon training or religious observances.

Slaughter also says "enlisting men" is key to the success of professional mothers, and that many more Generation Y-men actively think about how they will achieve work-life balance themselves because they were raised by working mothers, and "they understand 'supporting their families' to mean more than earning money."

– US News

> The trouble is not that I am single and likely to stay single, but that I am lonely and likely to stay lonely.
> - Charlotte Bronte

> The fear of being hurt in a relationship usually causes you to stay single or fear of getting attached to a person.
> - Anonymous

> I like being single, I'm always there when I need me.
> - Art Leo

Chapter 6
The Choice To Remain Single

One day a woman devotee requested the Holy Mother to order her daughter to marry. At this the Holy Mother replied:

"Is it not a misery to remain in lifelong slavery to another and always dance to his tune? Though there is some risk in being a celibate, still, if one is not inclined to lead a married life, one should not be forced into it and subjected to lifelong worldliness. Those girls that are drawn to the ideal of complete renunciation, should be encouraged to lead a celibate life."

On another occasion, the mother of a monk requested the Holy Mother to ask her son to go back to worldly life. The Holy Mother replied to her: "It is a rare good fortune to be the mother of a monk. People cannot give up attachment even to a brass pot. Is it an easy thing to renounce the world? Why should you worry?"

– From *Thus Spake the Holy Mother*

All of us agree with the idea that marriage is one of the most stable and fundamental bonds of civilised society. It promotes communities, develops lineage, links past with the future, and encourages parents and children to perpetuate valuable traditions nurtured through the institution of the family.

And yet, marriage is not for all!

Though most of the population of India and a considerable percentage of people in other countries of the world get married and set up families, yet the fact remains that many men and women (of late, in ever increasing numbers) choose to stay single.

Rather than generalise on reasons for the decline in marriages, let us stay focussed on the subject of this book, women. Why do many women choose to stay single these days?

From conversations with friends and reading books on women and society, I have gathered the following reasons:

1. They have not found this mythical person called "Mr. Right". In plain English, they have not found their ideal life partner, and are not willing to settle for anyone less than their chosen ideal. They are not miserable on that account either. They continue to be happy and single.

2. Many young women today feel that their career is more important than marriage or motherhood. Some of them feel that a family of their own might actually hamper their professional progress and growth. They stay single because they feel they cannot do justice to marriage and children.

3. The idea of 'freedom' and 'independence' are now consciously associated with staying single. Having one's own 'space' is highly valued now.

4. Many young people are growing increasingly disillusioned by the disintegration of values like loyalty, fidelity and staying true to a partner. They feel that marriage might be a risky proposition under such circumstances.

5. I know many young women who have stayed single because their family circumstances demand all their time and effort; by the time they are free of such obligations, it is too late for them to find a partner.

6. Many educated and intelligent young women choose to stay single because of evil practices like dowry, and are even more put off, when prospective in-laws become excessively 'demanding'.

7. Some young women are afraid of commitment. They are unable to accept the idea of sharing the rest of their lives and their homes and their time and their earnings with a partner over a lifetime.

8. Many young women are just happy to stay single! It is a deliberate and conscious choice they have made with open eyes. They are well

aware of the pros and cons of staying single; but they choose for themselves.

9. The idea of live-in partners (couples who choose to co-habit without the bond of marriage) is now gaining currency everywhere.

10. Many young women also choose to stay single for religious or spiritual reasons.

I would say these are both right and wrong, good and not-so-good reasons to stay single. May I also add, the last reason has always been the basis for several women down the ages, to choose a life of chastity and celibacy, as it has been with many men with similar aspirations. The monasteries and spiritual orders of the Roman Catholic Church like the Jesuits, Carmelites, Sisters of Charity and Franciscans as well as Hindu or Indian religious orders like the Ramakrishna Mission, Chinmaya Mission, · Brahma Kumaris and Sharada Math have had many committed women devoting themselves to the cause, renouncing worldly life and ties.

Apart from these, I also know several distinguished women in the field of education, medicine and social service, who have chosen to stay single, as their pursuit of perfection has left them with very little time or space in their personal lives for anything else. Such women are wedded to their cause.

My young friends tell me that the modern single women in the world's metro cities belong to a very different breed. Some of them are what we call 'hard core' professionals, who are determined to climb to the top of their profession or career, and regard marriage as; (1) too sacred and special to dabble with on a secondary status or (2) too demanding and restricting to permit them their desired freedom and growth.

Every one of us would agree that the entire idea of marriage is undergoing a sea change today. We have so-called 'long distance marriages' where the partners are working in two different places, and only get together for a vacation or on important occasions; we have 'weekend marriages' where the couple travel to be with each other at weekends; I am told there are wives who call themselves 'grass widows': their husbands are pursuing fast track careers which keep them away from home most of the time, and these women are 'single' in practical terms most of the time!

Many young women are also putting off marriage to a later age, despite the obvious parental pressure and worry. They like to stand on their feet, explore career and friendship as single women and then enter into marriage in their own good time. Gone are the times (at least in some social circles) when the parents could hasten the marriage of their daughters or even pressurise them to get married by 21 or 22 years, so that they (i.e. the parents) could fulfill their 'duty' or 'obligation' to 'settle' their daughters well.

"I am not an obligation to be fulfilled, a duty to be performed or a burden to be put down," says a young woman of my acquaintance. "I cannot be married off just because my parents have set a timeline for their tasks. I am a human being with my own aspirations and ideas. All I want is that they should be respected."

With increased educational opportunities and economic independence, many women simply turn away from marriage because the conventional notion of a man with higher education, better qualifications and higher status and income are no longer available for women who have attained to such a status themselves.

"We want to change the notion that marriage equals happiness," is the assertion of these women.

One possible result of this trend could be that 'communities' or groups of like-minded people might come to replace the family as a socially supportive structure for such people.

One point that we must all concede is that marriage is no longer an economic compulsion or economic necessity for a woman. She can choose to stay single or choose a life partner to her liking. She can choose the path of life that she wishes to tread.

There are many wise men and women who feel (very strongly) that Nature has endowed women with certain special attributes and gifts which are put to the best possible use as and when she becomes a mother. A career woman who chooses to stay single, will not be putting these gifts to the best possible use if she decides not to take on motherhood.

Gurudev Sadhu Vaswani too, once remarked that women could exercise the greatest possible influence on society as mothers, while men could maximise their influences as missionaries for any cause. A woman could contribute more to society through a family and children of her own, he felt. But, he added significantly, some women are born to be missionaries!

Though I am a great believer in the sanctity of motherhood and marriage, I feel equally strongly that they should not be imposed on anyone!

I cannot bring this chapter to a close without narrating to you the very significant episode from the life of one of the greatest *sanyasins* India has known – Sri Adi Shankara. Of course all of you are familiar with his name; but did you know the constraints under which he was forced to enter the marital state? It came to pass in the following manner.

In order to establish his *advaita* philosophy, Sri Adi Shankara had to challenge several well known scholars to a personal debate with himself and to prove the superiority of the *advaita* philosophy, he had to defeat them through logic and reason.

Mandana Mishra was one such scholar whom Shankara had to challenge. He was a leading proponent of the Mimamsa school, which emphasises the importance of rituals. He was very old when Shankara sought him out for a debate. But he had a very sharp intellect and a formidable grasp of logic. However, Shankara was already a realised soul. He had superior knowledge of Brahman, *maya* and *atman;* although their debate continued for six months, Mandana Mishra was forced to accept defeat at his hands, and decided to embrace *sanyasa* in atonement.

But Shankara's debate did not end there. Mandana Mishra's wife was an accomplished and spirited woman named Bharati, and she challenged Shankara to yet another duel of wits. Her contention was that in order to defeat a *grihasta* in debate, the opponent should also defeat his wife. "You do know that the sacred texts enjoin that a wife forms one-half of a husband's body (*ardhangini: ardha* – half; *angini* – body)" she said to Shankara. "Therefore, by defeating my lord, you have but won over only half of him. Your victory can be complete only when you engage in debate with me also, and manage to prove yourself better."

Having listened to the earlier debate attentively, she knew that she could not challenge Shankara's brilliance on weighty matters like Brahman and *maya*. Being a learned scholar herself and a very clever lady, and knowing very well that Shankara was a strict celibate, she asked him, "How can a *sanyasi*, who has no experience as a citizen and a householder, claim complete knowledge?" Forthwith, she launched into a discussion on husband-wife relationships and marital obligations. Shankara, realising that he could say nothing authoritative on these matters, asked for a recess of about fifteen days in the debate, so that he might be better equipped with knowledge on the subject. It was readily granted to him.

Shankara then used his *yogic* powers to enter the body of a king who had just died. The king who was given up for dead, seemed to revive miraculously and his two queens were delighted. In the meanwhile, Shankara had left strict instructions with his own disciples to preserve his deserted body very carefully. The renunciate's body lay lifeless in the care of the *shishyas*, while the subtle form of the *sanyasi* experienced the life of the *grihasta* in the form of the deceased king. Empowered with this knowledge, Shankara returned to resume the debate and defeated Bharati forcing her and her husband to accept *advaita* as their belief system.

The point I am trying to make is that even the greatest of philosophers, Adi Shankara, was forced to attain knowledge of the *grihasta ashrama* by subtle means, before his attainments could be complete!

For Your Reflection

"Single is not a status. It is a word that describes a person who is strong enough to live and enjoy life without depending on others."

– **Anonymous**

RABIYA

The name 'Rabiya' means beautiful. Beautiful was the life of Rabiya, although she was born to poverty and darkness; beautiful was her soul, for she walked the sufi way of devotion, love, detachment, humility, patience, gratitude and surrender.

Sold into slavery as a very young child, Rabiya faced hardship and privation which would harden the heart of any other girl; but this saintly soul bore her misfortunes with courage and fortitude. Her selfless spirit and her indomitable faith secured her freedom from slavery. Her deep devotion and intense faith worked miracles for her in her daily life, and she was worshipped as a saint, even in her lifetime. Yet she chose to live a life of poverty and simplicity, refusing all offers of financial support.

One day Rabiya was sitting on the banks of a river, meditating on the Divine. Dervish Hassan happened to pass by. Seeing Rabiya praying on the banks of the river he said to her, "Rabiya, why are you praying on the banks of the river? Let's offer worship to the Lord on the waters of the river." The truth of the matter was that Hassan had acquired extraordinary powers, whereby he could stay afloat on the water. He wanted to demonstrate his power to Rabiya and the world.

Confident of the spiritual power that could help him achieve miraculous feats, Dervish Hassan forthwith threw his prayer mat on the river. The prayer mat made of straw floated on the waters! "Come Rabiya," he called to her, "let's get on the prayer mat and offer our prayers to the Lord."

Rabiya was quite unmoved by the feat. She felt that it would only be a public display to impress people and not really an exercise in meditation. She said to Hassan, "If you want to meditate on God, I have a better way." Rabiya then threw her prayer mat in the air and said to Hassan "Come, let us rise in the air and meditate."

Hassan was mortified by Rabiya's gesture. He had actually wanted to make her admire his feats and powers; but she had overwhelmed him with hers. He said to Rabiya in all humility, "I cannot perform a miracle in air, for my *siddhi* (spiritual energy) is limited only to the water." To this Rabiya replied, "What you can do even a fish can do; and what I can do, a tiny fly can also do. But we are neither fish to float in the water, nor insects to fly in the air. Let us not forget the real purpose and the true goal for which we have received this human birth. These are mere tricks and we must not waste our precious human birth in working on them."

Rabiya received many proposals of marriage from rich men who were attracted by her radiant beauty. To them she said, "I have handed myself over to the Lord. If you wish to marry me, then ask God for me. If He should permit it, I shall agree, for my surrender to Him is absolute and complete."

Gurudev Sadhu Vaswani lovingly described Rabiya as the "Mira of Islam". She was indeed an evolved soul whose life was centered in God. Poverty and deprivation could not take away her essential goodness of heart and soul. A Mystic of the Divine, she lived the life of a true lover of God, accepting His Will in sorrow and happiness.

Rabiya's life and thought are eloquent testimony to the spiritual strength of womanhood.

I can promise you that women working together - linked, informed and educated - can bring peace and prosperity to this forsaken planet.

- Isabel Allende

Mothers always find ways to fit in the work - but then when you're working, you feel that you should be spending time with your children and then when you're with your children, you're thinking about work.

- Alice Hoffman

I feel very lucky because of my parents and then my education, the opportunities that I've had, so I would like to continue working to improve lives for others.

- Hillary Clinton

Chapter 7
Women At Work

"It's redundant to ask a woman if she is working," said a sister to me. "Being a woman is a twenty-four hour job."

She was right. As the proverb says, "A woman's work is never done".

A homemaker is like a CEO of the household – she handles finances; she deals with public relations; she is in charge of budgeting and planning; she deals with expenses and purchases; she handles social relationships and networks; she is in charge of domestic human resources; she is the trouble shooter, negotiator and the important collaborator for all new ventures that the family undertakes… and I could go on and on!

Let me say to you, that the above list does not just pertain to a typical upper middle class urban household. It applies as much to an educated, economically privileged wife and mother, as it does to a less affluent, economically backward group living in slums or in crowded *chawls*.

When we look at poor rural households, the situation is tough for a woman. Many of these women keep the household hearth lit by their strenuous personal effort – and I am not making a metaphorical reference, but a literal reference to their work. They go out to gather fuel, water and fodder everyday to light the *choolahs*, to cook food for the family and also feed their domestic animals. They cook, clean, take care of children and old people, and when household chores are at an end, they go out into the fields or into the brick kiln or smithy or whatever enterprise the husband works on, to assist him and give a boost to the family income. In their case, all of their labour is unpaid! Until recently, it was also invisible labour. That is, it went unrecognised, unrewarded, unrecorded. I am told that amends were made during the census of 2000, to take into account the women's contribution to the community and the family and only then were efforts made to quantify their labour and to appreciate the extent of their contribution to the nation's economy! Despite this effort, most experts agree that there is still a serious underestimation of women's work and the quantum of their contribution to the economy.

Many of these women in urban as well as rural areas are not permitted to go out and take a paid job. Technically, the man retains the title of breadwinner, while his wife becomes the unpaid domestic worker and caregiver.

In poor, urban social groups, a woman may be forced to go out and take up menial or domestic employment, when the man does not earn enough or worse, when he blows away much of his income on drinking and gambling and lotteries. In such cases, the mother or wife works a double shift at home and outside to bring food to her children. Whatever extra money she may have is often taken away by the man for his own expenses!

Under the circumstances, there is no such thing as a non-working woman; wouldn't you agree?

But we are talking here about women who have taken up jobs outside the home and are contributing to the family's finances.

For many women, there is a certain ambivalence in their attitude to work as in their attitude to marriage. The grass always seems green on the other side. Some working women are constrained by circumstances to take up a career; they long to be at home and devote time to their family and their loved ones. Equally, many homemakers envy their career oriented counterparts and long to be able to leave home every day and spend time in a friendly working environment.

Should women go out to work? Traditional, conventional, orthodox wisdom dictates that a woman's first and foremost responsibility is to her family and children.

Both men and women go to work outside the home these days. Man is no longer the "sole breadwinner" as he was earlier. The wife is also a "provider" now. But as a "provider" her responsibility is greater than his. Her role as a mother is crucial to the family and the future of the children. She, and only she can provide the secure, loving environment which is vital as the foundation for a child's life.

May I say to you, I am deeply saddened when I hear a woman say, "I am only a housewife." What she expresses in these words is the regret that she is not a working woman, not a professional, but someone confined to the four walls of the home. She does not know her real dignity and worth! If only she realises her onerous duties and responsibilities as a builder of the home, as the shaper of a new generation, as the architect of a new India, she would not refer to herself in such belittling terms!

But let us return to present circumstances – until recently, women were paid less for a full day's labour as compared to men, the assumption being that their contribution was less. Cheap female labour was thoroughly exploited in agriculture or horticulture, construction, road laying, quarries and labour intensive enterprises.

Ask the entrepreneur in any of these areas, and he will be the first to tell you that women are more dedicated and sincere in their work; they are more committed and need less supervision, and that he would prefer to hire women as they also come in as cheap labour!

In urban areas, the working woman has a visible presence. Apart from traditional areas like healthcare and education, women are also employed in corporate offices, manufacturing industries, IT and IT related sectors, garment manufacturing industries, software industries, banks, retail sector and other service industries.

Here are a few heartening facts: India has the largest number of professionally qualified women in the world; we also have a greater number of women doctors, surgeons, professors and scientists than the US. We have the largest female working population in the world! We have 'women achievers' in politics, sports, arts, education and entertainment. A few of them have actually made it to the top of their professional ladder and are showcased as symbols of women's empowerment and liberation. Economists and Market researchers will tell us that women now are earning more, having more money to spend and driving consumerism. But the ground reality is not so pleasant!

Working women face a multitude of problems on all fronts. Perhaps the most serious among them is that of Time Management. As I said to you earlier, they are literally working a double shift; working hard in the office and returning home only to take on their traditional duties of cooking, cleaning and care-giving. Friends tell me that in Mumbai suburban local trains, in the evening time, you can come across women returning home from work, who are actually cleaning or cutting greens and other vegetables, ready to be cooked when they reach home. This is just a small example of the way in which these brave ladies juggle work and family responsibilities.

At work too, they face discrimination, prejudice and sexual harassment. Despite legislation and protective measures, their safety and security are not ensured at the workplace or indeed on the roads.

Perhaps the most sensitive of these problems is care of children in the absence of mothers from home. Unfortunately, our traditional joint family system is no longer prevalent in cities. In effect, this means that grandparents are not around to ensure personal care for small children. On one level, the children are deprived of parental care; on a different emotional level, the working mother is traumatised by guilt and anxiety when she is unable to devote time to her children.

An understanding spouse and a supportive family structure are essential to a woman if she has to balance her home and her career successfully. Nothing, no paid help, no child support system, no baby minders can substitute for an understanding husband and caring elders!

When I speak about working women, who comes into your mind first? Many of the readers of this book are perhaps employing domestic help and I hope you think of these helpers also as working women! It is not just the professionals, the top income earners, the educated and affluent who belong to the category of working women. The so-called unorganised sector accounts for most of our working population and most women actually work in this category!

There are countless problems faced by working women of all classes and categories: transport, security, fair treatment and absence of discrimination, equal wages, unacceptable and at times unmanageable working hours, uncongenial working environments and the ever present fear of indignity and oppression in some form or the other...

I do not know whether the majority of these women would ever be counted as 'successful' in your terms; but each one of them, in her own way, has braved challenges, overcome obstacles and conquered deep inner fears and weaknesses to carve out a niche for herself in the world of work. Some of them, of course, have become legends in their lifetime, and are recognised by millions of their fellow countrymen as extraordinary achievers. Those who succeeded spectacularly, invariably had supportive families and loved ones; but the ones who are struggling with their lives need to be honoured and respected for their heroic efforts too!

For Your Reflection

Who has it easier when it comes to work-life balance: American professional women or their Indian counterparts?

There is no simple answer to this question. Many of the issues are common to women throughout the global corporate 24x7x365 work world of today: long work hours, challenging schedules, time-consuming commutes, need for childcare and eldercare support systems, the burden of household responsibilities, career path demands vs family demands, stress-related health problems and societal attitudes towards women and work. But the specifics differ due to policies, socio-economic and cultural differences.

Did you know that the United States is weaker in many of its statutory workplace policies for family than most of the other advanced economies and many emerging economies as well? The US is one of the few countries in the world that does not have federal laws guaranteeing paid maternity leave, paternity leave, a minimum number of paid sick days a year or the right to breast-feed a child in the workplace. Nor does the US have statutory entitlement to minimum paid holiday leave. Policies on these and other issues differ from state to state and from company to company. By contrast, India has progressive national laws and governmental policies in all these areas. The problem, however, is that the laws are not always rigorously enforced, and implementation is uneven.

On the plus side for Indian professional women is the availability of low-wage labour. Most middle-class Indian homes have either live-in servants or household help that comes daily to do cleaning, cooking and other household chores. In the US, this is a luxury available only to the upper-middle class. Another advantage in India is the support of the extended family system, whose network of mutual obligations can provide more practical help than the more atomised and dispersed American family. On the other hand, institutional resources for social welfare needs such as childcare and eldercare are more extensive in the US, infrastructure for commuting and flex-work arrangements is more advanced, and both food preparation and house cleaning are more mechanised.

The area in which the largest gap exists between the United States and India is in cultural attitudes about gender based work and family roles. Indian women have made enormous progress in higher education enrollment, workforce participation and career advancement within recent years, and many cultural attitudes are catching up with this new reality. For example, family objections to married women or young mothers working outside the home are diminishing. But attitudes towards the fundamental gender inequity that exists when it comes to housework, childcare and eldercare responsibilities (women's "second shift") have not changed significantly. The anecdotal stories one hears from Indian women about work-life balance issues circle around this cultural attitude but seldom directly challenge it.

**– Dr. Karine Schomer,
CMCT President and India Practice Leader**

MARIA MONTESSORI

The lady whose name we all associate with a liberal and lively mode of nursery education was an outstanding woman, for several reasons. She was not only the originator of a new system of children's schooling, but also the first woman in Italy to acquire a degree in Medicine.

Maria was born on August 31, 1870, to Allessandro Montessori and Renilde Stoppani. Her father was a retired army official from a wealthy and very conservative family. But her mother Renilde was a lively, intelligent woman, who encouraged her daughter to pursue her dreams, and supported her against strict social codes to take up a career of her choice. Although she was deeply interested in technical studies and mathematics and first enrolled herself in a technical institute in Rome, Maria discovered that she had a passion for medicine and decided to pursue her career in the same.

As things stood at that time, this was indeed a courageous, even daring move for the young lady. She was harassed and discouraged from pursuing medicine by fellow students as well as professors. The general opposition to her move only made her more determined to fight for equality, and it was a proud moment for both mother and daughter when she qualified to be a doctor in 1894, having specialised in pediatrics and psychiatry during the last two years of her degree course.

During her very first appointment as an assistant doctor at the Psychiatry Clinic in the University of Rome, Maria had the opportunity to work with disabled children, and she came to realise that what they needed most was not so much medical care or psychiatric treatment, but a different approach to teaching and learning. Her next position was as Head of the Orthophrenic School in Rome, where she had to care for "hopelessly disabled" and "highly idiotic" children, as they were referred to in offensive terms, in those days. Her teacher trainees studied anatomy, neurology and psychology under her to care for their differently abled students. She developed her own highly unique, successful and innovative methods to teach them, and the stint proved to be invaluable for her and the children. She was at the same time modifying, refining and adapting her methods to suit the young learners. At the end of this posting, she decided to pursue further research into this area.

In 1897, she was invited to address the National Conference of Medicine in Turin, where she spoke on the problems of juvenile delinquency. She urged the state to offer special schools and teaching methods for mentally disabled children, along with special training for their teachers.

She was made Head of the state supported school in the San Lorenzo area of Rome, where some of the city's poorest and most disadvantaged children came to study. Maria Montessori created a new environment for them in her school. For the first time, small sized tables and chairs were used in classrooms instead of severe looking desks and benches. The teacher began to assume the role of a guide or instructor, who was present in the background, while encouraging the children to freely pursue their creative ideas. Rigid lesson plans and heavy curricula were replaced by free learning using the five senses and the active curiosity of the child. The joy of work was its own reward. While the whole learning environment was free, it also had the effect of inculcating self-discipline in the children. Each child was treated as an individual in his own right, with his own unique gifts and abilities. The children enjoyed complete freedom of movement and work during their 'practical' sessions, when they cleaned and dusted, did a bit of gardening and helped each other put on aprons. This became famous as the Montessori method.

Maria now began to create materials for her classroom, in the form of picture cards and letters cut out from cardboard which the children loved using. She was also training teachers in the new Montessori method.

Her work now began to attract international attention. The first Montessori school in New York, USA, was opened in 1911. Many American teachers travelled to Italy to train under her, and Mr. and Mrs. Graham Bell, (inventor of the telephone) opened a Montessori school in their hometown in Canada.

Over the next twenty years or so, Maria Montessori travelled extensively across Europe, propagating her teaching methods and training new teachers. Spain, UK and Netherlands were among the first countries in Europe to adopt her methods. Gradually, Montessori schools were also established in France, Germany, Switzerland, Belgium, Russia, Serbia, Canada, India, China, Japan, Indonesia, Australia and New Zealand. Rabindranath Tagore who was then establishing his own Shanti Niketan, was one of her earliest supporters, and helped to set up the Montessori Association of India. She was also invited by the Theosophical Society of India to come and deliver a few lectures at various colleges in South India.

She was nominated for the Nobel Peace Prize. Montessori was also awarded the French Legion of Honor, Officer of the Dutch Order of Orange Nassau, and received an Honorary Doctorate of the University of Amsterdam. Till her last years, she continued to travel and lecture all over Europe as well as in Asia.

Maria was almost eighty-two when she died in Noordwijk, Holland in 1952. She had become a legend in her own lifetime.

We can no longer enshrine a patriarchal culture
nor condone violence with attitudes at the
expense of our women.

- Steve Swart, MP, South Africa

Women are the only oppressed group in our society
that live in intimate association
with their oppressors.

- Evelyn Cunningham

In passing, also, I would like to say that the first
time Adam had a chance, he laid the
blame on woman.

- Nancy Astor, My Two Countries

Sure God created man before woman. But then you
always make a rough draft before the
final masterpiece.

- Author Unknown

Chapter 8
Changing Attitudes Towards Women

> 50 years ago men viewed women as someone to protect, to care for, to cherish, to worship, to love.
>
> Certain women wanted more and felt that there was a better way, where women would be just like men, and do the exact things men do.
>
> So, since men were forced to view women as smaller men, men have lost the desire to protect, care for, cherish, worship and love women.
>
> Now women complain that men don't protect them, care for them, cherish them, worship them or love them like they used to.
>
> Kind of ironic isn't it?
>
> – Source: Unknown

It is said that Maha Pajapati Gotami, Gautama Buddha's aunt and stepmother who brought him up and cared for him after the early demise of his mother, approached the Buddha and asked to be received into his *sangha* and become a nun (*bhikkhuni*) along with a few of her friends. Initially, so Buddhist scriptures tell us, the Buddha refused.

However, Gotami was not to be put off. She and hundreds of her followers cut off their hair, dressed themselves in monk's robes, and set out on foot to follow the Buddha who was moving from place to place.

One day, Ananda, the Buddha's cousin and most devoted attendant, found Pajapati in tears, dispirited, exhausted, her feet swollen. "Mother, what is wrong? Why are you crying like this?" he asked.

Gotami appealed to him to talk to the Buddha and allow her and her friends to be inducted into the *sangha*. Ananda promised her that he would definitely speak to the Master on their behalf.

Ananda kept his word. Sitting at the Master's feet, he asked why women should not be ordained to become nuns attached to the *sangha*. The Buddha would not agree to his request, until Ananda placed before him the question: "Was there any reason why women could not realise enlightenment and enter *nirvana* as well as men?"

The Buddha was forced to relent. "No, that is not the case," he replied. "Women, Ananda, having gone forth are able to realise the fruit of stream-attainment or the fruit of once-returning or the fruit of non-returning or *arahantship*."

Forthwith Gotami and her followers were permitted to become *bhikkhunis* and enter the *sangha*. But very harsh and strict measures were laid down for the women as against their male counterparts in the *sangha*; and the Buddha added what was to become perhaps his most controversial statement against women: he remarked that allowing women into the *sangha* would cause his teachings to survive only half as long – 500 years instead of a 1,000 years.

There are people who say that the Buddha's predictions proved to be right: Buddhism failed to strike deep roots in India. There are people who argue that the predictions proved to be wrong; 2500 years after his death, the world still remembers and reveres the Buddha's teachings.

Why did Gautama Buddha make the kind of statement which is interpreted by many as misogynistic? Was the Buddha really skeptical about women and their spiritual aspirations?

Some scholars say that the Buddha was concerned that the rest of society, which supported the *sangha*, would not approve of the ordination of nuns. Ordaining female disciples was a revolutionary step in those days; there was nothing like it in the other religions of India at the time.

Or, they say, the Buddha might have simply been protective of women, who faced great personal risk in a paternalistic culture when they were not under the protection of a father or husband.

Swami Vivekananda, at the state of highest realisation, said that he saw the presence of the Divine Mother in all women. He worked tirelessly for the upliftment of women, saying: "The best thermometer to the progress of a nation is its treatment of its women," and again, "There is no chance for the welfare of the world unless the condition of women is improved."

It is truly inspiring to hear his impassioned defence of the equality of the sexes, citing nothing less than the Vedas as the ultimate authority: "It is very difficult to understand why in this country [India] so much difference is made between men and women, whereas the Vedanta declares that one and the same conscious Self is present in all beings. You always criticise the women, but say what have you done for their upliftment? Writing down *Smritis,* etc., and binding them by hard rules, the men have turned the women into manufacturing machines! If you do not raise the women, who are a living embodiment of the Divine Mother, don't think that you have any other way to rise!"

Mahatma Gandhi was not only the Father of our nation, the architect of our independence; but he was also a great social reformer. He fought spiritedly to eradicate the wrongs committed against the women of the country through the ages. His political ideology was strongly anchored in humanitarian values, and reflected his deeply spiritual nature.

Not only did Gandhi bring about a general awakening among the women, but also brought them boldly out into the national mainstream, standing shoulder to shoulder with their fellow Indians in the Satyagraha and Quit India Movements. Gandhi asserted: "To call women the weaker sex is a libel; it is man's injustice to women." Indeed, he played a stellar role in uplifting the status of women in India.

Gandhi had the greatest respect for Indian culture and traditions. But he was determined to root out those practices which were detrimental to the progress of women. So he remarked, "It is good to swim in the waters of tradition, but to sink in them is suicide." Some of these 'traditions' he fought against were child marriage, the treatment of widows and the custom of dowry. He thought of these practices as being evil and immoral. He openly appealed to girls not to marry men who demanded dowry, at the cost of their self respect and dignity. He appealed to young men to come forward to marry young widows. For Gandhi, the *purdah* system was no less than a "vicious, brutal and barbarous" practice. The predicaments of the *devadasis*, a part of the lower, untouchable segment of the society, touched his heart profoundly. He left no stone unturned for rehabilitating this segment of the society. He often said that one of the first tasks that needed to be accomplished as soon as the country won freedom was to abolish the system of *devadasis* or temple women and brothels.

He often cited the examples of ancient role-models who were epitomes of Indian womanhood, like Draupadi, Savitri, Sita and Damayanti, to show that Indian women could never be feeble. Women have equal mental abilities as that of men and an equal right to freedom. To sum up in Gandhi's words; "The wife is not the husband's slave but his companion and his help-mate and an equal partner in all his joys and sorrows – as free as the husband to choose her own path."

Now, I must turn to my own Master, Gurudev Sadhu Vaswani. He was truly a great visionary, philosopher and saint whose life was a saga of service and sacrifice for the betterment of society, the upliftment of women and the welfare of the poor and the downtrodden. At the same time, he was also aware of the dangers of excessive 'modernism', warning women against aping western fashions blindly. He encouraged them to cultivate the virtue of simplicity in their dress and in their daily life. And Simplicity would be the first of the steps that took them forward to the spiritual path.

This spiritual aspect of women's unfoldment was foremost in his mind, when he turned his attention to women's education. The MIRA Movement in Education, which he founded in Hyderabad-Sind, set new standards for value-based education which emphasised character development and cultivation of the soul. His ideal of the triple training of the head, the hand and the heart added a new dimension to the education of girls. His innovative practices did not end there. For the first time in modern Sind, he offered hostel facility to girls who could not have access to good education in the vicinity of their homes. When he founded Mira College in Sind, he had it affiliated to the Banaras Hindu University, arranging to send the girl students with appropriate escort and security to Banaras, for their University exams.

Rightly has it been said, that if you educate a man, you educate an individual; education contributes to his individual growth; it becomes his 'private property', as it were. But when you educate a woman, you educate the entire family!

Therefore, did Gurudev Sadhu Vaswani describe the woman as the symbol of *shakti*. This *shakti* is not physical force, but the power of integration. And to the development of *stree shakti*, he devoted his vision of the Mira Movement in Education.

I have spoken of great and distinguished souls and their views on women. There have been many other great patriots who have fought for the cause of their sisters: Raja Ram Mohan Roy, Ishwar Chandra Vidyasagar, Jyotiba and Savitribai Phule, Swami Dayananda Saraswati and others. But what is the reality that confronts us today?

We live in troubled times today. You do not have to go on the internet to become aware of the atrocities against women that are happening all over the world. You don't have to switch on your TV to watch news broadcasts, which are full of such violence against women; you don't even have to turn the pages of the newspaper to keep track of what's happening. The people you meet at work, the commuters who travel with you, even the stranger you meet on the street, everyone is talking about the latest act of violence – until a new horror pushes it aside.

MARY MAGDALENE

The name of Mary Magdalene is mentioned in the New Testament versions of Mark, Matthew and Luke, as one of the foremost female disciples of Jesus Christ. Her role in these canonical gospel may be small – but it is of special interest to all scholars who seek to learn about the role of women in early Christianity, as well as in Jesus's ministry during his lifetime.

Mary Biblical traditions identify her with Mary, the sister of Martha; some say that she was a sinner who was forgiven by Jesus; however, the Eastern Orthodox Church holds her as a distinct figure, a great woman saint of the Catholic Church.

Gurudev Sadhu Vaswani read not only the canonical scriptures but also the independent chronicles and narratives of those times to weave the beautiful story of her life into one organic whole.

Mary Magdalene was a woman of affluence, who lived a life of pleasure. When she first beheld Jesus, she was overwhelmed by the fragrance of his holiness, the beauty of his purity and the power of his love for all living beings; above all, she felt the power of his aspiration to unfold the divinity within each man and woman who came unto him.

Jesus looked at Mary Magdalene and he saw into her sins, her lapses and her failings, her faults, her repeated retreats from the path of purity and virtue. But he also saw that in her fallen, sin-scarred life, the shadow of God's grace, the Light of the Eternal.

Her next meeting with Jesus was dramatic. The Pharisees dragged her before him when he was addressing a crowd. They said to him, "This woman has sinned and we have caught her in the act. We bring her to you, for you claim you are a Prophet of God. Under the Law of Moses, she must be stoned to death. We would stone her, but not until you permit us to do so."

Jesus looks at Mary, and then at the Pharisees. Ever so gently, he tells them, "Let him, who is without sin among you, throw the first stone at her."

The Pharisees are stunned; they dare not cast the first stone; their arrogance disappears. One by one, they slink away.

Jesus asks Mary, " Where are the men who brought you? Hath no one condemned you?"

Mary answers, "They are all gone!"

Jesus tells her, "Neither do I condemn you. Woman, go and do not sin again!"

Mary's life is transformed. She is determined to lead a clean, pure, sinless life now.

We have other accounts of Mary in the apocryphal gospels. Non-canonical gospels such as those of Philip, Thomas and the Acts of Peter portray her as a thinking disciple – someone who often asked intelligent questions when the other disciples were confused by Jesus's teachings and his new philosophy. In fact, these versions record that Jesus had a special place for her in his affection, because of her wisdom and understanding.

In later Christian Iconography, she is most often portrayed in acts of devotion to Jesus – washing Jesus's feet, anointing him, or sitting at his feet to listen to him. It was she who discovered the empty tomb of Jesus after his resurrection, and was bidden to inform the other disciples of the same. In fact, John says that after his rise from death, it was before her that Jesus first appeared.

Was she the penitent sinner forgiven by the grace of Jesus? Or was she the intelligent, independent disciple who supported his ministry with her personal wealth, and rose to become one of his beloved disciples? Whosoever she might have been, her fame lives on to inspire the faithful. Her story is the beacon of hope for all men and women who have stumbled and fallen in sin, but aspire to repent and move onward, Godward.

The sad truth is that our mothers, sisters and daughters are no longer safe in our sophisticated, technologically advanced and evolved society of the twenty-first century.

What has become of the values and ideals that Swami Vivekananda, Mahatma Gandhi and Gurudev Sadhu Vaswani left behind as their legacy to us? Why have we become so degraded as to descend to a society that fails to respect its women and treat them well?

Sociologists would give us many reasons for this change for the worse: they would probably tell us that women are still regarded as sense objects, as inferior creatures, as man's 'property' and 'goods' to be bought or sold or treated as he pleases; feminists would probably blame the degraded male mentality which cannot bear to see women walking free and fearless as equal partners in this enterprise of life; yet others would say that it is a deep rooted orthodox mindset that we have failed to fight over centuries.

A news report from the Middle East was brought to my notice and it read: "Dowry deaths, female infanticides and sexual molestations are words that are heard time and again in India."

These may be sensational; but there are other mundane problems faced by our women that don't make headlines: malnutrition, maternal mortality, poor health care facilities, over work, lack of education and lack of power to make their own choices – these are issues that affect the lives of many underprivileged women.

I began this book by talking about Maitreyi and Gargi; I cannot pretend that I am unaware of what is going on in 2013, as this book nears completion.

Where are we headed? How can we mend our ways and repair the tattered moral fabric of our society?

For a Change... The Good news!

The lives of women around the world have improved dramatically, at a pace and scope difficult to imagine even 25 years ago. Women have made unprecedented gains in rights, education, health and access to jobs and livelihoods.

Despite the progress, gaps remain in many areas. The worst disparity is the rate at which girls and women die relative to men in developing countries. Excess female deaths account for an estimated 3.9 million women each year in low- and middle-income countries. About two-fifths are never born due to a preference for sons, a sixth die in early childhood, and over a third die in their reproductive years.

The World Development Report 2012: Gender Equality and Development published recently, argues that closing these gaps is a core development objective in its own right. It is also smart economics. Greater gender equality can enhance productivity, improve development outcomes for the next generation, and make institutions more representative.

The analytical core of the Report constitutes a conceptual framework that examines the factors that have fostered change and the constraints that have slowed progress. The analysis focuses on the roles of economic growth, households, markets, and institutions in determining gender differences in education and health, agency and access to economic opportunities.

The analysis leads to the identification of four priority areas for domestic policy action:

- Reducing excess female mortality and closing education gaps where they remain

- Improving access to economic opportunities for women

- Increasing women's voice and agency in the household and in society

- Limiting the reproduction of gender inequality across generations

AUNG SAN SUU KYI

Among the great leaders of People's Movements in the last six decades, three names stand out: Martin Luther King Jr.; Nelson Mandela and Aung San Suu Kyi. What they had in common was this: that they followed Mahatma Gandhi's philosophy of *ahimsa* or non-violent resistance. The Myanmar woman leader Suu Kyi has won international recognition and appreciation for her determined fight to bring democracy to her people.

Aung San Suu Kyi derives her name from three relatives: "Aung San" from her father, "Suu" from her paternal grandmother and "Kyi" from her mother Khin Kyi. Her name might sound difficult, but it is known to millions of people worldwide, who admire her for her courage, fortitude and conviction.

Suu Kyi was the third child and only daughter of Aung San, considered to be the father of modern-day Burma. Her father was responsible for bringing about Burma's independence from British colonial rule. But he was assassinated before independence became a reality. The day he died is still observed as National Remembrance Day in Myanmar, as the country is called today.

Brought up by her mother, Khin Kyi, Suu Kyi accompanied her mother to India when the former was appointed as Burma's ambassador to India. She graduated from Lady Sri Ram College, New Delhi, before she went on to pursue higher studies from Oxford and New York and other international centres of learning. In late 1971, Aung San Suu Kyi married Aris, a scholar of Tibetan culture, living abroad in Bhutan. Sadly, he died of cancer, when his wife was under house arrest in Myanmar.

Suu Kyi first entered politics to work for democracy, and founded the National League for Democracy on

September 27, 1988. Within a year, she was put under house arrest by the ruling military junta. She was offered freedom if she left the country, but this she refused.

One of her most famous speeches was *Freedom From Fear*, which began: "It is not power that corrupts, but fear. Fear of losing power corrupts those who wield it and fear of the scourge of power corrupts those who are subject to it."

She also believes fear spurs many world leaders to lose sight of their purpose. "Government leaders are amazing," she once said. "So often it seems they are the last to know what the people want."

Amnesty International declared her as "a prisoner of conscience". For over fifteen years, she remained under virtual arrest, separated from her husband and two sons. She could not be by the side of her husband, when he died of cancer in 1999. Indeed, Aung San Suu Kyi paid a heavy price for the sake of her people and her country. It was only in 2010 that she was finally released from house arrest.

During her prolonged house arrest which was followed by continuous military surveillance and restricted movement, Suu Kyi received several awards, including the Sakharov Peace Award and the Nobel Prize for Peace. But it was only on June 16, 2012, that she was finally able to deliver her Nobel acceptance speech (Nobel lecture) at Oslo's City Hall, two decades after being awarded the peace prize.

Even today, when international pressure has forced the military dictatorship to release her, it is not clear whether her heroic struggles will bear fruit in terms of true democracy for her people. But the world will surely remember this noble, courageous woman as a heroine who confronted a fierce opposition without taking up arms against them or resorting to any form of violence. Indeed, Aung San is one of the most beloved icons of the twenty-first century.

We hold these truths to be self-evident, that all men and women are created equal.

- *Declaration of Sentiments, First Women's Rights Convention*

Somewhere out in this audience may even be someone who will one day follow in my footsteps, and preside over the White House as the President's spouse. I wish him well!

- *Barbara Bush, Former First Lady of the US*

One is not born a woman, one becomes one.

- *Simone de Beauvoir*

Women who seek to be equal with men lack ambition.

- *Timothy Leary*

Chapter 9

The Special Qualities Of The Woman Soul

Someone said to me the other day, "Dada, are you sure that the new generation of women value and wish to imbibe the ideals that Gurudev Sadhu Vaswani placed before them? Do they not need to fight for their equality and rights in a world that has placed obstacles on their path, handicapped them and put them at a serious competitive disadvantage?"

I smiled at his question. "Do you think Gurudev Sadhu Vaswani did not choose the right ideals? Or perhaps, you think that these ideals are outdated?"

"No, no, Dada, of course not," the friend hastened to intervene. "What I meant was that the great thinkers and leaders of our country like Gurudev Sadhu Vaswani and Swami Vivekananda have undoubtedly placed noble ideals before us; but they were men of their time, conditioned by their time... To expect women today to imbibe their ideals might be a little difficult, perhaps even unacceptable to women themselves..."

"Please forgive me Dada," he added as an afterthought. "I certainly do not have the wisdom to question these great ideals. But I thought that a clarification from you might help me understand them better."

"I feel the same, Dada," said a sister who was part of the group. "Let me add this, I am amazed at the courage and conviction with which you speak of these ideals before audiences in India and the West, knowing how different and so very modern some of the women are!"

"Let me put it to the test," I said to our little group, "What are your views on the ideals I seek to promote?"

After an initial period of silence, one of the members spoke up. "Well, Dada, none of us can deny that they are lofty, noble ideals. But don't we also want our daughters to grow up to be accomplished, successful individuals, achieving the best that they are capable of, fulfilling their highest potential?"

Another sister added, "I have sometimes wondered, Dada, if we are not overburdening, overtaxing our women with too high expectations that might actually impede their progress."

An uncomfortable silence fell over the group. I realised that it was my turn to speak, and to dispel doubts.

Perhaps there are some of you who are reading this book, who feel the same way as these brothers and sisters did. Times have changed; humanity has moved on; and therefore, it is time we changed our values and ideals?

Let me reiterate those ideals that Gurudev Sadhu Vaswani emphasised:

- Simplicity
- Sympathy
- Service
- Purity
- Sacrifice
- Spirituality
- *Shakti*

He said that these were the special qualities of the woman-soul. These were special feminine energies, beautiful female vibrations that emanated in the spirit. Would you not agree that these are also universal attributes to be nourished, cherished and inculcated in all of us as human beings?

Then why are these qualities held up to be the special attributes of a woman, you might ask.

The answer to that is twofold: As I explained earlier, the woman-soul is NOT a term that relates to gender. It refers to aspects of the soul, the *atman*. We all have female and male energies within us. When there is a perfect balance of these energies, we have an ideal human being.

ST. TERESA OF AVILA

St. Teresa was born in Avila, Spain, on March 28, 1515, one of ten children and the daughter of a Toledo merchant and his second wife. Her mother Beatriz was determined to raise her daughter as a pure Christian, and would often narrate stories of the lives of saints to her in her childhood days. Such was the impact of these stories on Teresa's vivid imagination, that at the age of seven, she ran away from home with her brother Roderigo, to become a martyr among the Moors. The children were spotted by their uncle just outside the city walls and brought back home.

When Teresa was 14, her mother died, plunging her into profound grief that prompted her to grow emotionally close in deep devotion to Virgin Mary, the mother of Christ, whom she began to regard as her own spiritual mother.

With her mother dead and her elder sister married, there was no one to take care of Teresa at home; and she was entrusted to the care of Augustinian nuns in a convent, where she settled down after initial pangs of separation from her family. She grew in greater love and devotion to God, and chose a religious life over marriage.

Having joined the Carmelite convent, Teresa took to the habit of mental prayer, establishing a link of communication with God from her heart. As she herself would say later, "Prayer is an act of love, words are not needed. Even if sickness distracts from thoughts, all that is needed is the will to love."

During this period too, she was subjected to severe illness which almost left her crippled; but she survived with the grace of God. She also experienced several mystic visions which left a deep spiritual impression upon her.

In those days, life in the Carmelite Convent was far

from ideal; a spiritual malaise seemed to prevail over the inhabitants; the main concern of the superiors was to raise money for the convent; to this end many young girls from affluent families were taken in as novitiates, although they did not have the calling. It is recorded that some of these young nuns wore jewellery and took great pains about their appearance, especially when it was time to receive visitors to the convent. The prevalent atmosphere was worldly. There were floods of visitors, many of them young men, whose frivolous conversations and vain pursuits only vitiated the atmosphere. All this had a detrimental effect on Teresa's spiritual progress. She longed for solitude and silence, and resolved that she would form an order where the rules would be far more stringent, with a return to the more ancient ideals of primitive simplicity, poverty and prayer, so as to stop such violations of the sanctity of the cloister.

This was not a move welcomed by the existing order. When her superiors at the convent heard of her plans, they denounced her and ordered her to raise funds for them; they even threatened her with the Inquisition. The town started legal proceedings against her. All this only because she wanted to try a simple life of prayer! Despite the mounting opposition, Teresa was undeterred by the threats and hostility; she just went ahead calmly, trusting absolutely in God.

In 1562, she established her own order at San Jose. This was the new order of the Discalced Carmelites, or Barefoot Carmelites, a Catholic mendicant order with roots in the eremitic tradition of the Desert Fathers and Mothers. At first she had little support and very few resources; there was also bitter opposition from rival orders and the general public. But the local Bishop and senior Jesuit monks supported her initiative, and this was followed by a papal sanction, along with royal grants from the King of Spain.

Her rules for the new Order were as follows: a life of continual prayer, safeguarded by strict enclosure and sustained by the asceticism of solitude, manual labor, perpetual abstinence, fasting, and fraternal charity. It was also to be an Order fully dedicated to poverty.

Inspired by Teresa's example, St. John of the Cross also set up a similar order for men. Despite the stringent rules, men and women of devotion flocked to the new Order, not only to take up religious life, but also to learn the habit of true and sincere prayer.

Her writings, produced for didactic purposes, stand out among the most remarkable in the mystical literature of the Catholic Church. They include her *Autobiography*, *The Interior Castle* and *The Way of Perfection*.

From the year 1567, she began to undertake long and arduous journeys through the whole of Spain, to set up new houses of her order, under patents from the Carmelite Order. Her reform convents were established at several centres in Spain during this period. She continued founding these institutions until her death in 1582.

In 1622, forty years after her death, she was canonized by Pope Gregory XV. The papal honor of Doctor of the Church, was bestowed upon her by Pope Paul VI in 1970, making her one among the first women to be awarded the distinction.

Most of our wise men agree that it is due to the predominance, indeed, an excess of male attributes like aggression, power and violence that human civilisation has been scarred by wars and strife. Therefore, to go back to where I started in this book, "Man has had his chance. Now it is the turn of the woman." Attributes like compassion, understanding, sensitivity and harmony must be cultivated – not just by women, but by all of us, so that tragic mistakes of the past are not repeated.

Now, to turn to the second part of my answer: Why do I seek to encourage my sisters to cultivate these qualities especially? Why do I emphasise those qualities like motherhood and nurturing which, perhaps, some of them are rejecting, or perceiving as regressive?

Dear readers, motherhood and nurturing are not just gender attributes or biological traits. Mother Nature has blessed women with the great gift of the maternal instinct. Every great woman is equipped to become the role model, the source of inspiration, the fountainhead of *atmic shakti*, heroic energy to all mankind.

"We do not want to become mothers of heroes, we want to be heroic ourselves," exclaimed a sister, at one of my question-answer sessions.

I have no quarrel with that aspiration! My dearest wish is that all of us may become truly heroic, in the way Gurudev Sadhu Vaswani and Swami Vivekananda visualised.

The patron saint of our MIRA Movement in Education was not a biological mother. But we hold her in veneration as a heroic soul. And even today, parents are proud to name their daughters after her. The Blessed Teresa and sisters of her order took vows of celibacy and chastity; and we love to call them Mothers.

I repeat: every heroic woman is blessed by God to be a mother, a nurturer of humanity. It is undoubtedly great to be heroic; but it is far greater to inspire others to become heroic!

I am not being anti-women when I glorify motherhood; my ideas on the subject will become clear to you when I tell you that I often like to invoke God in His Mother aspect! I feel that is His special and unique relationship with me, by means of which I can approach Him freely, without fear and hesitation, and in the certainty that He will hear my prayers and shower me with His grace!

If we (as indeed all Hindus) can endow God with the traits of a Mother, how can such an attribution be demeaning or belittling?

If people are apt to say that Indians worship the woman as Mother and then violate her dignity and self-respect in deeds of daily life, the fault is not with the ideal, but with the imperfect human beings who fail to translate the ideal into practice!

In the sections that follow, let me share with you my views on enlightened, inspiring, uniquely female qualities of the woman-soul: they are meant to empower and elevate you; not saddle you with impossible burdens. These views are shared with my sisters for their inspiration and empowerment. If my brothers are also inspired to emulate them, they will be truly blessed. For being a woman is to be ennobled, chosen for a mighty role in shaping the future of human civilisation as things stand today. If men wish to stand shoulder to shoulder with them in the cause of reconstruction and reconciliation, I can only say that they will be privileged to be equal partners in the task. Let me reiterate too, my unshakeable faith in those ideals and my unbounded reverence for the great Master and Visionary Prophet who gave expression to them!

Here are some characteristics of a godly woman – check off the ones that describe you:

Gracious, Virtuous, Sober, Chaste, Prudent, Discreet, Peaceable, Patient, Kind, Faithful, Joyful, Good, Merciful, Pleasant, Ready, Honourable, Benevolent, Quiet, Spiritual, Modest, Obedient, Loving, Inspiring...

Now before you get discouraged, understand this – I know that we fail in different areas on this list from day to day ... but we should NOT look at this list as a reminder of our failures but instead with HOPE, OPTIMISM and ANTICIPATION of what we have to look forward to. God will help us to become these things. We cannot do all of this in our own strength. It is only because of Him that this can take place and we must remember that God has not finished His work in us yet!

– June Fuentes, *A Wise Woman Builds Her Home*

MIRA

Mira's very name spells music and devotion; from her immortal songs wafts the fragrance of *Krishna Bhakti*, devotion to the Lord. Princess and ascetic wanderer, Rajput noblewoman and self-exiled free soul, Mira carved out her own path to Liberation, as very few women had dared to do before her.

Mira was born around 1499 A.D. She was the daughter of Rana Ratan Singh Ranthor, a brave Rajput prince and spirited warrior, who died on the battlefield, fighting Mughul invaders. At a very young age, Mira went to live with her grandfather, Dudaji, in Merta.

The Ranthors of Merta were devout believers in Lord Vishnu. Thus Mira grew up in an atmosphere of intense piety and devotion.

It is said that as a small child, Mira once witnessed a marriage procession, with a richly attired bridegroom, the *dulha*, as the centre of attention, the cynosure of all eyes. So impressed was the little girl that she ran to her mother and asked her in all innocence, "Mother, who is my *dulha*?"

Smiling indulgently at the child, Mira's mother replied, pointing to an image of Sri Krishna, "Here he is, your own Giridhar Gopal."

Whether she meant it as a joke or whether she meant it in earnest, who can tell? But from that day onwards, Mira never ever forgot that He was her beloved, her *dulha*, her own Giridhar Gopal. She began to regard herself as Sri Krishna's bride.

Mira's family did not take her devotion seriously. Following the Rajput tradition, they arranged her marriage when she was still very young. The chosen bridegroom was

Rana Bhoj Raj, scion of the Royal family of Chittorhgarh. To him was Mira married, with all pomp and splendour. When she left for her husband's home, she was sent with the dower that was due to a princess; but all that Mira treasured and took with her was the little statue of Sri Krishna that she had loved and worshipped as a child.

According to some accounts, Mira was a dutiful wife, who did not neglect her household duties. But other accounts reveal that she was reluctant to worship the household deity of her husband's family, and insisted that her devotion was reserved only for Sri Krishna.

Around this time, many parts of Rajputana came under attack from the Mughul sultans of Delhi. In the ensuing struggle between the warlords of Delhi and the fiercely independent Rajput clans, many brave princes lost their lives, Rana Bhoj among them. Around this time, Mira also lost her parents and several of her family members. Perhaps these tragic events taught the young maiden to turn away from the transient, temporal world of material reality and focus her attention on the Eternal. Filled with the spirit of *vairagya* (detachment) she began to spend all her time at a little shrine of Krishna, that her husband had built for her. Day and night, she sat at the feet of her Beloved Sri Krishna, singing songs in His praise.

Brought up as the darling of her family and married into one of the noblest Rajput royal clans, Mira chose to turn her back upon the worldly life as a Rajput queen and the routine domesticity of her traditional marriage to seek the goal of Union with God, her Beloved Giridhar Gopal. Her society and her times were far behind her in thought and vision; they utterly failed to understand her. As for her *bhakti,* they were incapable of appreciating anything so intense and so fiery - for lip service and rituals were the limits of their own worship. But confined as she was by the limitations and restrictions of her social and familial environment, Mira's spirit could not be curbed or confined. Her chosen role was that of the servant to her Lord; her avowed aim was to surrender her all at His Lotus Feet. What could stop such intense devotion?

The Royal traditions of the Chittorgarh clan into which she was married, expected her to live the life of seclusion and isolation – or else commit *sati* by immolating herself on her husband's funeral pyre, when he was killed in a battle.

Her brother-in-law, Vikramjit Singh, who had now become the ruler, was displeased by her behaviour, which, he thought, was unbecoming of a Rajput queen. Adding fuel to his fire of wrath was his sister, Uda Bai, who indulged in wild and malicious gossip about Mira. Mira's ever growing popularity among the masses, the great love and reverence in which the people held her, was also a thorn in his flesh. He commanded her to stop dancing and singing in the temple; her reply is in the form of a song whose words are now etched in our hearts:

Dyed deep am I in the colour of Shyama
To whom I am consecrated,
Dyed in the colour of Krishna am I.

I put on my anklets for the love of Shyama
I dance before my Giridhara
Mira is dyed deeply in the colours of Hari.

Day after day, Mira faced persecution and psychological pressure from her husband's family. She bore it all in patience, with undaunted courage. In every difficulty and crisis that she faced, her only support and solace was her devotion to Sri Krishna.

The Rana continued his persecution. Once he sent a

serpent to the temple; in its place, she found a bunch of flowers for her *puja*. Uda Bai sent her a cup of poisoned milk; the vicious poison had no effect on her at all! Soon, there came a stage when Mira decided that she should leave her worldly confines behind her, once and for all. She left Chittor, and set out as a wandering ascetic in search of her Lord.

The princess turned into a *bairagin,* a homeless wanderer.

Gurudev Sadhu Vaswani tells us, that it is ever the fate of those who aspire to meet the Lord, that they must face loneliness; they must tread their chosen path all alone.

This princess who became a wandering minstrel, sang her way into the heart of India – and indeed into the heart of Dwarakanath, the Lord of her devotion. She merged with the Divine – but her songs live on, as immortal as the divine flute melody of Sri Krishna!

Mira's songs live on! And she lives on too, in the hearts of all Indians, like the flute of the Lord!

There is no greatness where there is no simplicity, goodness and truth.

— Leo Tolstoy

I do believe in simplicity. It is astonishing as well as sad, how many trivial affairs even the wisest thinks he must attend to in a day; how singular an affair he thinks he must omit. When the mathematician solves a difficult problem, he first frees the equation of all incumbrances, and reduces it to its simplest terms. So simplify the problem of life, distinguish the necessary and the real. Probe the earth to see where your main roots run.

— Henry David Thoreau

Possessions, outward success, publicity, luxury - to me these have always been contemptible. I believe that a simple and unassuming manner of life is best for everyone, best for both the body and the mind.

— Albert Einstein

Chapter 10
Simplicity

Simplicity is not a way of life favoured by many of us in this materialistic generation. Yet the great Founders of world faiths, Messiahs and Prophets like the Buddha, Jesus Christ, Prophet Mohammed and Guru Nanak lived lives of utter simplicity. The *rishis* of ancient India, Christian saints who built up the great monastic orders and the Sufi saints of east and west held up the virtue of simplicity in practice. Mira and Avvaiyar turned their back on luxuries and wealth and chose to live lives of austerity. But, as Richard Gregg, the author of *The Value of Voluntary Simplicity* tells us: "Our present 'mental climate' is not favorable either to a clear understanding of the value of simplicity or to its practice. Simplicity seems to be a foible of saints and occasional geniuses, but not something for the rest of us."

There is a beautiful Kabir *Bhajan* which I have heard soulfully rendered by the late Purushottamdas Jalota. Here is a rough translation of the song:

> *How can your mind and mine be at one?*
> *I tell you what I have seen with my eyes. You speak of what is written in texts.*
> *I say 'simplify' but you complicate.*
> *I say 'stay awake', but you sleep.*
> *I say 'be detached' but you get attached.*
> *For long have I urged you to listen, but you pay no heed to me.*
> *You gamble and lose all your money.*
> *The grace of the* Satguru *flows pure and clean.*
> *Cleanse yourself in that current*
> *Then, says Kabir, you too will become pure.*

JANA BAI

Jana Bai was not born to wealth and prosperity. She was not literate, for she had not received the benefit of formal education. She could not even read the alphabets, leave alone the *shastras*, or the scriptures. But to this day she remains one of the most loved saints of Maharashtra.

She was born in what people thought of as a lower caste. When she lost her mother at a young age, her father took her to Pandharpur, where he left her in the house of a well-to-do tailor known as Dhamasheti, as a domestic servant.

Dhamasheti and his wife Gonai, were deeply religious. At the time Jana came to work for them, their son Namdev was just a little younger than the servant girl. It was Jana who attended to most of the needs of this boy, who was to become one of the greatest saints of the land.

Jana was blessed to live in the environment of this pious household. She did all the household work, but her heart was always with Vithoba. Many times while working, sweet, melodious songs poured forth from her lips. Often, while grinding grains or washing clothes, she called out, "Vithal! Vithal! Many years have passed by, but still I have not had a vision of You."

She was unschooled; practically illiterate; but her poetic talent which was steeped in true *bhakti*, was phenomenal! Some of Janabai's songs suggest a life of difficult labor in the household, but one that was constantly revived and supported by the strength and power of her intimacy with the Divine:

> When Jani sweeps the floor
> her Lord gathers up the dirt.
> When she lifts the wooden pestle
> He cleans the mortar stone.
> He doesn't stand on dignity
> He collects cow-pats by her side.
> When she goes to fetch the water
> her Lord follows after.

Janabai's songs, her *abhangas* are considered as the priceless treasure of Maharashtra. Even today, in many houses and temples, her songs are sung with great enthusiasm and devotion. Your eyes will go moist with tears when you listen to her *bhajans*, because they are not merely made up of words, they portray the grief of the aspiring soul and its pure devotion.

She was blessed to be in the house where it was her duty to serve a saint like Namdev. Perhaps it was God's plan that the two saints' lives should be so intertwined! Janabai had the golden opportunity to look after Namdev and care for him in his childhood. The many saints and realised souls who came to visit Namdev were also associated with the humble devotee of the Lord, Janabai. She was herself a great soul, a saint-in-the-making; but she was content to regard herself as Namdev's servant – *Naamyasi dasi*, as she herself put it.

In several poems on devotion which she has left behind, she describes herself as "Nama's maid-servant" or "Namdev's Jani". She was one of the closest followers of Namdev and had no ambition other than to serve Namdev and sing the praises of the Lord Vithoba. For instance, in one of her poems she sings:

Let me undergo as many births in this world as You please, but only grant this – that my desires are fulfilled.

And this is my desire – that I see Pandharpur and serve Namdev in every birth.

Let me be a fowl or a swine, a dog or a cat, but in each of these lives, I must see Pandharpur and serve Namdev.

One day, she had to grind a huge quantity of jowar. That night, after everybody went to bed, she began to grind the grain; and as she toiled over the *chakki*, the philosophy of life poured forth from her lips:

My lovely grindstone
how sweetly it spins
as I sing your praise.
Come to me, Lord.

Twin poles of World and Spirit
smooth wooden handles
my five fingers grasp by turns.
Come to me, Lord....

The grindstone of life
grinds me down like grain.
I gather and pack the flour.
Come to me, Lord.

Spirit heats the vessel
the scum of sin boils over
the broth of virtue clears.
Come to me, Lord.

As the grindstone stops, says Jana
so will I one day. When I go
my fame I'll leave behind.
Come to me, Lord.

It is said that her Lord, Panduranga was so impressed and touched by her devotion and her philosophical rendering of the truth of life, that He came and sat next to her and helped her in her task. He sat beside her, and as they took turns to grind the grain, they discussed various aspects of human life and its struggles.

The day broke and the voices of devotees were heard from a distance. Janabai hastened to bid goodbye to the Lord and urged Him to return to His sanctum sanctorum, before He was missed by the priests at the temple, and the early morning worshippers. As for the Lord, in His hurry, He left behind His silken shawl and His jewellery beside her and covered Himself with her rug, as He left in a hurry.

When the priests opened the doors they were astounded! All the jewels of the deity were missing and in their place was an old, torn rug. Somebody identified it as Janabai's rug. Immediately the priests lodged a complaint against her. A search warrant was issued. The temple authorities rushed to her house – and, sure enough, the Lord's jewels were found beside her grinding stone! She was arrested immediately and the death sentence was passed against her. Namdev's pleadings fell on deaf ears.

Very soon, the day of her execution dawned. She was dragged along the streets to the public execution venue. She was badly injured and bleeding, but nobody cared. She begged the officers not to drag her along, but it was of no avail. Finally she was brought to the gallows. Her few friends and followers wept bitterly for her but her detractors and a few self-seekers gloated over her misery. Little did they know, that the 'low born' maidservant whom they despised, was one who was favoured by the Lord Himself. What does the Lord care about wealth and power and high birth and breeding? For Him, she was a dear devotee, a chosen soul. God chooses such pure souls as His own for their *bhakti*, for the pure love of their hearts, but not for their caste or creed.

Turning to the people who were gazing at her, all agog with curiosity, she asked them, "Why have you gathered here? Is this a pleasant spectacle for your entertainment? O, idle folks, go and utter the name of the Lord, for He alone can save you!"

The dreaded noose was placed around her neck. She was about to be hanged. The name of Panduranga rose in the air and echoed into the sky. The onlookers could not believe their eyes! The rope disappeared and in its place was a beautiful, fragrant garland of flowers around her neck. Janabai was filled with joy. The self-seekers hung their heads in shame.

The *abhanga* written by Saint Namdev appropriately sums up Saint Janabai's greatness –

Janiche Abhanga lihit Narayan | karit shravan sadhu sant |
Dhanya techi jani, dhanya tichi bhakti | Namdev stuti karitisi | |

(Jani's *Abhangas* are composed by God himself | all the saints listen to her religiously | Blessed is Jani, blessed is her devotion | Namdev so praises her | |)

Janabai took the straight and simple way to attain God. She walked what Gurudev Sadhu Vaswani called "the little way": the way of simplicity, humility and service. She did her work and fulfilled all her duties; but while doing her work, while fulfilling her duty, she never ever forgot Him! His name was ever on her lips! His vision ever dwelt in her heart! And she was indeed richly blessed.

Many of us are apt to equate happiness and success with money, material wealth and possessions; and I blame it on our materialistic culture. It is for the women to lead the movement that will take us in the other direction. People cannot be happy just because they live in mansions or penthouse apartments. They cannot achieve peace and inner harmony just because they drive expensive cars. They cannot be considered 'successful' just because they are millionaires.

Driving a Benz or a Porsche does not make you a better person. Flying to Europe or the Bahamas for a vacation does not add to your inner sense of worth. Diamonds, gold, rubies, stocks, shares and mutual funds do not always guarantee peace and harmony in your life.

Alas, many of us regard these outer 'symbols' as indicators of our happiness and success. These material resources are not as valuable as our inner, personal resources.

Let me say to you, I think we are beginning to complicate our lives unnecessarily, perhaps unintentionally – with excessive acquisitions and unnecessary possessions. But the worst thing is that we tend to ignore, forget or take for granted things that should really matter to us! I recall a statement made by the writer Perroux: "The whole value of life comes from things that have no price."

Ramakrishna Paramahansa considered simplicity essential for success in spiritual life: "There is a sect of *Vaishnavas* known as the *Ghoshpara* who describe God as the '*Sahaja*', the 'Simple One'," he said to his followers. "They say further that a man cannot recognise this 'Simple One' unless he too is simple."

We are told too, that Sri Sarada Ma taught a little girl how to adopt simplicity in life: "Do not demand anything of those you love. If you make demands, some will give you more and some less. In that case you will love those more who give you more and those less who give you less. Thus your love will not be the same for all. You will not be able to love all impartially."

To my sisters who are reading this book, I make an appeal: do not measure your love for your husband in terms of what he earns and what he gifts you with! Do not make such demands on him that he is forced to adopt dishonest means just to satisfy your wants. Above all, teach your children that money is not everything!

Simplicity is a divine quality, and women must be the first to cultivate it, so that men may learn its value from them. Simplicity in living; simplicity in thought, word and deed; simplicity in approach and in problem solving...

Let me offer you the example of the Quakers, who believe that a person's spiritual life and character are more important than the quantity of goods he possesses or his monetary worth. They also believe that one should use one's resources, including money and time, deliberately and consciously in ways that are most likely to make life truly better for oneself and others. Their 'testimony to simplicity' includes the practice of being more concerned with one's inner condition than one's outward appearance and with other people more than oneself.

Is this not an ideal worthy of our emulation? Simplicity and modesty in attire never ever go out of fashion. Excessive use of jewellery and ornaments not only appears to be exhibitionistic, it also raises issues of safety.

There is also the issue of simplicity in thought and expression: Nowadays, we come across so many people who speak not just to communicate or to express themselves, but to display their scholarship or even their polished accents! They don't just speak; they pronounce their opinions more to impress others rather than express their views. There are others who use words to terrorise, threaten, coerce and browbeat those around them!

Nowadays we reject the old view that a soft voice suits a woman. But is it not true that a woman can do more to persuade through love and gentleness than by threat or coercion?

Beyond expression, there is also the simplicity of faith and acceptance: the firm belief that all that happens to us need not be analysed and rationalised threadbare to find complicated reasons, (except when we have made mistakes that need to be corrected) but accepted as the Will of God. Excessive questions in the vein of "Why me?" or "What have I done to deserve this?" can be replaced by the simpler response: "How can I deal with this situation?" or "What are the lessons I must learn from this incident?"

Many women entrepreneurs and corporate leaders will also tell you that they have adopted the unclutter-reduce-simplify attitude to solving problems. They would also urge us not to complicate issues with excessive emotions.

It is women who must take the lead in cultivating simplicity. I am deeply pained when I see the ostentatious and lavish wedding functions that are now becoming a habit with some of our families. Expensive buffets are laid out, and much of the food heartlessly wasted or thrown away in a country where millions of people can't get even one square meal a day. Loud, blaring music and crass display of wealth distract our attention from the deep and profound significance of the wedding rituals. More often than not, these grand 'celebrations' are condemned as obscene displays of wealth – a harsh reminder to all of us that we should stick to the essentials and avoid such extravagance.

We live today in an age of "Conspicuous Consumption" – i.e. the acquisition of goods not out of necessity, but out of the desire to 'show off' our wealth and status. The distinguished economist Thorstein Veblen who first studied this phenomenon, predicted that the price of ostentatious goods would go upwards, while people would simply reject low-priced options. We are witnessing the Veblen effect even now!

Simplicity Misplaced

I can't find simplicity these days. It's lost — buried somewhere beneath all my stuff. Well, I suggest that it's time for me to dig up this misplaced virtue. Of course, it's been so long since I've seen it, I might not know what to look for. So, as I rummage through the piles of my possessions, here are some of the things I might want to keep my eyes open for.

- Simplicity is not buying a bigger house only because my best friend just bought one.

- Simplicity is not getting the newest gadget just because it is the newest gadget.

- Simplicity is not taking the job with twice the salary if it means that I'll have to spend half the time with my family.

- Simplicity is increasing the amount I give away, rather than skyrocketing my standard of living, when the Lord blesses me financially.

- Simplicity is recognising the difference between necessity and luxury, and choosing to do without the luxuries, because so many in our world lack the necessities.

To state the matter plainly, simplicity means living an uncluttered life. Simplicity is the path less travelled because there is less on the path, and if you are like me, you are prone to prize possessions. But where greed and covetousness say, "I must possess more," simplicity says, "I am content with what God has given."

– Dillon T. Thornton

For Your Reflection

Simplicity is freedom from duplicity, affectation or pretension. In dress, food, character, style, manners, in all things the supreme excellence is simplicity. There is beauty and majesty in simplicity. It is nature's first step and the last of her arts.

Be what you say and say what you are. Write as you speak and speak as you think. Be simple like a child. The door of *moksha* will then be opened to you.

– Swami Sivananda

LALITA SHASTRI

Her husband was famous as one of the very few politicians in India who made no money. Today, Mrs. Shastri also is remembered for the same sincerity, simplicity and austerity that characterised their personal and public life.

People like Mr. and Mrs. Shastri do not belong to the glamorous celebrities that the world dotes on. But they belong to a rare breed of public figures who stood for the greatest values and ideals of this land.

Lalita Devi of Mirzapur married the young Lal Bahadur in 1928. In a strong but silent protest against the prevailing tradition of hefty dowry, Shastri accepted only a *charkha* and a few yards of *khadi* as dowry.

Young Lalita decided to improve her Hindi with tuitions. She paid the tuition fees by dispensing with the domestic maid and doing the household chores herself. Her husband would often hand over to his wife his *khadi kurtas* when they became unusable and ask her to make handkerchiefs out of them. He taught her to live on the simple philosophy of 'waste not, want not'.

But Lalita's married life was not an easy one. In 1930, her husband threw himself into the freedom struggle during Mahatma Gandhi's Salt Satyagraha. He was imprisoned for two and a half years. Once, while he was in prison, one of his daughters fell seriously ill. He was released for fifteen days, on the condition that he would not take part in the freedom movement. However, his daughter died before he reached home. It is said that the family could not afford to buy the costly medicines that had been prescribed for her. After performing the funeral rites, he voluntarily returned to prison, even before the expiry of the period of bail.

A year later, he asked for permission to go home for a week, as his son had contracted influenza. The permission was given, but his son's illness was not cured in a week. In spite of his family's pleadings, he kept his promise to the jail officers and returned to the prison.

His biographers say that this was the period in his life, when the family lived in abject poverty, literally not knowing where the next meal would come from. Many years later, as Prime Minister, he would tell his administrative officers that he knew what poverty was, and reveal the story of those days when he lived on Rs. Two and a half per month! As a Minister, when he lived in spacious bungalows, he refused to be corrupted by the affluence of his new status, and stuck to his simple way of life.

Lalita shared with her husband all the trials and tribulations of life that had to be faced by an honest and dedicated freedom fighter. Shastri spent nine years of his life in jail. During these spells, Lalita looked after the children and household. The family moved to New Delhi in 1952 when Shastri became the Railway minister. When he resigned his post as a result of a railway accident, they walked out of their bungalow. When he quit the cabinet under the Kamaraj Plan, he always paid his own bills. He was Prime Minister for all too brief a period, before he died tragically. Once again, Mrs. Shastri quit the official residence allotted to him. But Indira Gandhi allotted the house to Lalita Shastri, and she lived there till her death in 1993.

Although Shastri had been a cabinet minister for many years in the 1950s, he was poor when he died. All he owned at the end was an old car, which he had bought with a bank loan from the government and for which he still owed money. The loan was repaid by his widow out of her family pension.

Lalita Shastri was a brave and courageous woman who always stood by her husband's side; she shared his ideals of integrity, honesty and sincerity; she made no demands on him and provided him with her moral support and commitment in his effort to uplift the life of the common people of this country.

No one has yet realised the wealth of sympathy, the kindness and generosity hidden in the soul of a child. The effort of every true education should be to unlock that treasure.

- Emma Goldman

Pity may represent little more than the impersonal concern which prompts the mailing of a check, but true sympathy is the personal concern which demands the giving of one's soul.

- Martin Luther King, Jr.

If men and women are to understand each other, to enter into each other's nature with mutual sympathy, and to become capable of genuine comradeship, the foundation must be laid in youth.

- Havelock Ellis

Who can tell what metals the gods use in forging the subtle bond which we call sympathy, which we might as well call love.

- Kate Chopin

Chapter 11
Sympathy

Sympathy is one of the most sensitive and delicate of human virtues. It would not be far too wrong to say that it is one of those qualities that make human beings human. It is that innate capacity that some of us have to respond appropriately to an emotional situation. Nor is sympathy an instinctual reaction; at its highest form, it operates in conjunction with conscience and reason, forming the very basis of a human being's moral components, and therefore enabling a human being's moral evolution.

I am not a specialist or scholar to enter into debate with psychologists and sociologists on whether sympathy is innate, instinctive or an acquired emotion! I cannot give you a discourse on the nature of sympathy; but I can tell you that I have seen and felt and experienced sympathy in action! It is the capacity of the individual to reach out to share the joy and pain of others. It is innate, but we can acquire the emotion of sympathy from the habitual behaviour of the people we are close to; the gift of tears, like the gift of laughter, is contagious. Just as we smile in tune with other smiling faces, so too, we shed involuntary tears at the sight of sorrow or suffering; as that beautiful expression in English puts it, our hearts go out to others!

I cannot help thinking that the quality of sympathy is also closely related to our imaginative capacity; for it is only when we enter imaginatively into the feelings and suffering and sorrows of another person, when we put ourselves in the other person's shoes, as it were, that we respond to the situation with sympathy.

Let us pause to reconsider some of the words I have used to talk about sympathy: sensitive, innate, instinctive, emotional, imaginative – are not these attributes specially those which we associate with women?

ANNIE BESANT

Annie Besant (1847–1933), was described as a 'Diamond Soul', for she was a woman with several brilliant facets to her character. She was an independent thinker, an intelligent seeker of truth, an outstanding orator of her time, a champion of human freedom, educationist, philanthropist, and author with more than three hundred books and pamphlets to her credit. She showed the way for thousands of men and women all over the world in their spiritual quest.

She was born Annie Wood, to a middle class Irish family in London. She was proud of her heritage and supported the cause of Irish self-rule throughout her adult life. When her father died, the family was left in dire straits. Her mother decided to take on boy students from Harrow as boarders. She could not look after her child, and entrusted Mary who was just five years old at the time, to the care of her friend, Mrs. Ellen Marryat. Marryat made sure that Annie received a good education. She also imbibed from her guardian a strong sense of duty to society and an equally strong sense of what independent women could achieve.

At 19, Annie married the young Rev. Frank Besant, and within four years they had a daughter and a son. But gradually, Annie's views began to change. She tells in her autobiography that in her role as a minister's wife she tried to help her husband's parishioners who were in need, but she came to believe that in order to alleviate poverty and suffering, deeper social changes were needed beyond immediate service.

Annie became increasingly radicalised in her political views; whereas Frank was generally conservative, Annie instinctively supported the rights of workers and poor farmers. Annie also began writing, but her husband didn't allow her to keep her earnings. More seriously Annie began questioning the religion of her birth and in 1873, she stopped receiving Communion because she no longer felt she could call herself a Christian. Her husband ordered her to leave their home, and they separated permanently.

Her life now changed completely. She became an activist for freedom of thought, women's rights, secularism, birth control and the rights of the working class; she was also highly critical of the influence and teachings of Christianity, especially its orthodoxy, its persecutions and religious oppression.

By now, she developed a reputation as an outstanding public speaker. Here is what one of her listeners had to say of her: "Mrs. Besant transfixed me; her superb control of voice, her whole-souled devotion to the cause she was advocating, her love of the down-trodden, and her appeal on behalf of a sound education for all children, created such an impression upon me, that I quietly, but firmly, resolved that I would ascertain more correctly the why and wherefore of her creed."

Annie became increasingly concerned about workers and their plight; when she heard about the health of young women workers at the Bryant & May match factory, she published an article entitled "White Slavery in London" in which she drew attention to the dangers of phosphorus fumes and condemned the low wages paid to the women who worked at Bryant & May. She helped the women to form a Match girls Union. The company was forced to improve working conditions in their factory.

After years of political and ideological change, a great spiritual change came over Annie, when she was exposed to the work of Madame Blavatsky, whose book, *The Secret Doctrine*, she was asked to review.

She became a supporter of Theosophy, a religious movement founded by Helena Blavatsky in 1875. Theosophy was based on the profound Hindu ideas of *karma* and reincarnation. Under the influence of this movement, she went to live in India. She took a great interest in women's emancipation and also became involved with the struggle for Indian Home Rule. This British born free thinker was actually interned by the British authorities for supporting the nationalist cause. She also helped to establish the Central Hindu School and College, which later became the Banaras Hindu University, led by Madan Mohan Malaviya. She constantly worked to secure women's rights and equality for the lower castes. Her efforts were also directed towards rejuvenation of the *panchayati* system.

She also prepared *The Lotus Song*, a translation of the Gita into English and gained recognition for this achievement. She claimed that she was a Hindu of the ancient type, and felt a great kinship with the spiritual ideals of India.

On September 25, 1915, she announced her decision to set up a Home Rule League. Congress rejected her Home Rule programme. Nevertheless she opened up various branches for her movement to flourish much to the British government's dislike.

She was made President of the Congress' Calcutta session of 1917. She moved the most crucial resolution passed at the Congress' Amritsar session (1919-20), namely that on the Jallianwala Bagh massacre, with a scathing attack on the officials responsible for the episode.

In the last 13 years of her life, she moved away from active participation in politics.

We can say that with her inborn sympathy for the causes that were dear to her, she achieved a rare feat: recognition as an 'Indian' woman leader at a period of great turmoil even while being a white woman.

In the nineteenth century, female moral superiority in sympathy and service was almost a given in western society. This is why women like Florence Nightingale were acknowledged and given due recognition when they took to the work of healing and caring for the sick. Indeed, healing and helping come naturally to women, don't they?

Today, women physicians and women doctors occupy a position that men cannot really occupy and wield an influence that men cannot hope to match! And this is not just in specific areas like gynaecology or physiotherapy, but in diverse other areas like oncology, ophthalmology and radiology, where their attitude, their emotional responses and their entire professional approach enable them to offer a major alternative kind of treatment!

A recent study undertaken in the US found that women doctors reacted more empathetically with their patients, prescribed milder drugs and showed greater concern with their patient's social and psychological condition than their male colleagues. They also took far more interest in preventive medicine.

We would all agree too, that the impression made on young minds by their kind and understanding teachers lasts a lifetime! Many middle aged people may not remember the professors in College who taught them Botany or Chemistry, but virtually every one of us is bound to remember the kind and loving teacher in the Nursery or KG class who taught us to sing and dance and clap, and stopped us from fighting with our peers!

Don't get this wrong: I am not trying to tell you that women doctors and teachers are the only ones who are the outstanding examples of sympathy. The point I'm trying to make is that sympathy (whether it is an emotion, an instinct or a social attitude) comes naturally, spontaneously to women.

"What you leave behind is not what is engraved in stone monuments, but what is woven into the lives of others," said the Greek thinker, Pericles. Women weave beautiful patterns in the lives of the people they touch with their sympathy, compassion and understanding.

You cannot be sympathetic unless you are able to rise above selfishness and begin to care for others. In this sense, sympathy is getting involved with others, reaching out to others, becoming aware that we are interdependent as human beings. Sympathy is making a selfless, worthwhile contribution to others' lives; and as that remarkable woman Eleanor Roosevelt puts it, "When you cease to make a contribution, you begin to die."

Does this not remind you of the words of Gurudev Sadhu Vaswani which I love to repeat again and again; "Those who give, live; for those that give not are no better than dead souls."

When I say give, giving is not restricted to cash or cheques or donations in kind; the attitude of giving, the impulse with which you give matters as much, if not more than the actual quantum of what you give. And giving comes naturally, spontaneously, instinctively to women and children.

I appeal to all women: let your sympathy extend to all suffering humanity; but above all, let your sympathy extend to your own sisters, other women! It hurts me to hear people say, "Women are their own worst enemies," or "Women perpetrate the greatest cruelty against members of their own sex," etc. A leading spiritual Guru has actually said: "A woman's only form of relationship with other women is that of jealousy." Perhaps he was trying to provoke them into breaking the pattern; perhaps he wanted them to refute his claims. Whatever his motives, he was stating an unpalatable view which many people hold to be true!

Therefore, be sympathetic to your sisters!

Today, many feminists argue that men have been conditioned to suppress true emotions like pity and sorrow, to their own detriment. "If men are not meant to cry or shed tears, why do they have tear glands?" is a question that is often heard in feminist debates. Women, as we know, break into tears spontaneously; they are not afraid, not reluctant to respond with their hearts. How I wish we could all learn from them!

How is it that women are more spontaneous, more sympathetic than men? It goes back to the root cause I spoke to you earlier: women are ruled by the heart. Their logic and reasoning are directly related to their hearts. This is why compassion, sympathy, caring and the gift of tears come so naturally to them.

As selfishness, cruelty, violence, aggression and hatred are threatening to overwhelm modern sensibility, we need to reassert the qualities of sympathy, compassion, benevolence and sensitivity so that the darker, brutal forces that threaten our civilisation are kept at bay, and a sense of balance and harmony are restored in the world. Men need to be educated, trained in these qualities; it is the mother, the wife and the daughter who can instill these qualities in them.

A sister said to me the other day, "Women for centuries have been told they have a particular place in society. It is for them to practice compassion, listen, understand and extend a helping hand and an understanding heart. But women need to be more self-sufficient and independent today. How can they go on empathising, living to listen to others and caring for them?"

I said to her, "It is not for the woman to take on the role of silent sufferer and burden bearer all the time! It is time for her to train men in the finer arts of understanding and compassion. If she doesn't teach them, no one else will!"

In this, as in other matters, the responsibility we place on women is high! But this does not absolve the rest of us from emulating her example.

BERTHA VON SUTTNER

History highlights what it wants to and throws its veil over some facts and people and events. While history has told us enough and more about Alfred Nobel and the Prizes named after him, not many of us know about Bertha von Suttner, who was his secretary for a short time, who influenced his decision to move away from his flourishing dynamite business and devote at least some of his fortune to more constructive activities. The rest, as they say, is history that is much better known. Our purpose here is to throw light on this remarkable woman who had the opportunity to influence a historical event and did so successfully.

She was born Bertha Kinsky, an Austrian noble woman, who later became an author and peace activist. She came to work as a secretary for Alfred Nobel in Paris in 1876. After only a couple of months she left her job and returned to Vienna to get married. But she maintained an extensive correspondence with her former employer and was quite outspoken about the military applications of the deadly merchandise that he dealt with, namely dynamite. She worked very actively for the peace movement in Austria and Germany. Among her books is a classic *Die Waffen nieder* (Lay Down Your Arms) published in 1889. She also published a pacifist journal with the same name.

In her life-long correspondence on peace matters with Alfred Nobel she urged him to establish a prize for peace. This led to his endowment in his will for prizes to be given each year for achievements in physics, chemistry, medicine and physiology, literature, and for work toward peace. Nine years after Alfred Nobel's death, Bertha Von Suttner was awarded the Nobel Peace Prize in 1905, the first woman to be thus recognised.

(The following incident from Holy Mother's life has been recorded in *Sri Sarada Devi and Sri Sarada Math*, published by Sri Sarada Math.)

A woman who had taken a wrong path was rejected by her family. Holy Mother gave her refuge, and attracted by Mother's love and sympathy, the girl began to come to her often. However, women from respectable families did not look upon the girl with favour. Golap-Ma argued with Mother, "Mother, don't allow this girl to come here. You are not able to tell her, I will."

Mother calmly said, "How can this be? She will come to me. She is my daughter."

A much respected woman devotee said, "If she comes, we will not come."

When Mother heard this from Golap-Ma, she said in a firm voice, "If she doesn't want to come, she won't come. If anyone doesn't want to come, let them not come. But she will come to me. Everyone has someone; she has no one but me. She will be with me. I will not prevent her from coming because someone will not come if she does."

Everyone was astonished to hear these words from Mother. Holy Mother is the Mother of everyone: the fallen, the tramped-upon and the oppressed.

Man can never be a woman's equal in the spirit of selfless service with which nature has endowed her.

-Mahatma Gandhi

As far as service goes, it can take the form of a million things. To do service, you don't have to be a doctor working in the slums for free, or become a social worker. Your position in life and what you do doesn't matter as much as how you do what you do.

- Elisabeth Kubler-Ross

I am only one, but still I am one. I cannot do everything, but still I can do something; and because I cannot do everything I will not refuse to do the something that I can do.

- Helen Keller

Service is the rent we pay to be living. It is the very purpose of life and not something you do in your spare time.

- Marian Wright Edelman

Chapter 12
Selfless Service

All of us at the Sadhu Vaswani Mission are personally acquainted with the spirit of selfless service in women. When Gurudev Sadhu Vaswani decided to begin his first school in Hyderabad-Sind, all he had was just a two-paise coin; the Bank of Providence took care of the rest. But, as we all know, it is not just money which builds a school! Devotees, volunteers and philanthropists came forward to help him. A core fund was quickly established. Able, willing, well-qualified women devotees offered their services free, to teach and work in the school — in the same spirit of service and sacrifice urged by the saintly founder. This is how the first Mira school came into being.

The spirit of selfless service is what the world needs desperately today. Everyone is so obsessed with 'I' and 'Mine' that there is no one to think about 'us' and 'them'; nobody to grieve for common human suffering; no one to extend a helping hand where there are going to be no returns on investment except a smile of gratitude and a heart filled with appreciation!

The spirit of selfless service! If I had a million tongues, I would appeal to you with each one of them, especially to my young friends who are going to be tomorrow's leaders and opinion makers — seek not power! Seek service! And I firmly believe that the selfless attitude of caring and sharing comes naturally to women!

Therefore, I urge my sisters to take the lead, in this as in other aspects of life that matter. Let us do as much good as we can, to as many as we can, in as many ways as we can, on as many occasions as we can and as long as we can!

How can the world be peaceful and prosperous if one fraction of its people lives in luxury and opulence while the majority live in poverty and deprivation? Therefore, we must all learn to share what we have with others! Let us set apart a portion, say one-tenth of our earnings, to be utilised in the service of God and His suffering creation. Charity and service begin at home, and who but our mothers and homemakers can take the lead here?

To some of us, who are unable to make two ends meet or live within their income, this may at first appear a very difficult thing to do! But we will find eventually, that in the measure in which we share what little we have with others, we will be truly blessed – and this world will be a better place for our humble endeavours!

Many of us are ready to love and sympathise with those who are close to us – relatives, friends, loved ones. We may go out of our way to help them, but when strangers are involved, do we rush to their help, or do we simply turn away? *This* is the true test of compassion.

The shortcut to world peace and prosperity is through love, compassion, service and the spirit of caring and sharing. It is also the shortest and quickest route to God. The way of service is closely allied to the way of kinship with all humanity – for we need to assert, again and again, "I am my brother's, my sister's keeper!"

And who are our brothers and sisters? Our brothers and sisters are all those who suffer and are in need of help – men, women, birds and animals. We must become channels of God's mercy, help and healing, so that His love may flow out to them through us and our actions. When we become instruments of God's love, there is no limit to what we can accomplish. In God's Divine Plan, we can become the sanctuary of the weary and heavy-laden; we can, with our efforts, become a source of sweet, refreshing waters in the wilderness that is this world.

It hurts me to have to say this: we are now living a life of isolation and alienation that denies this sacred kinship with the rest of humanity.

FLORENCE NIGHTINGALE

The guiding star of the care-giving profession, a pioneer among women as the finest Nurse and Medical Worker, Florence Nightingale is remembered the world over as 'The Lady with the Lamp'. Indeed, she lit the lamp of healing, selfless service and devotion to duty, dispelling the darkness out of the lives of the wounded soldiers of the Crimean War of the nineteenth century. She laid the very foundations on which the Nursing Profession is built. Even today, our young nurses take the Nightingale Pledge, in her honour. The Annual International Nurses Day is also observed on her birthday.

Florence was born in a cultured, affluent upper class family, and named after the city of her birth – the beautiful city of Florence with its glorious tradition of art and architecture. She had the best of everything – but she broke away from the restrictive conventions of the Victorian Society to follow her calling – that of a healer and helper of men.

She could have settled into the comfortable, lethargic life of an upper class wife and mother; in fact, she even received several proposals from desirable young men; but she felt she had a 'Christian calling' to enter the nursing profession. Braving family opposition and anger, she worked hard to educate herself as a nurse – and laying the foundation for nursing education in the future.

Her mission of help and healing was extended to people living in poverty, and wounded soldiers in distant lands, hospitalised in the most unsanitary conditions. She was the first to point out that the hygiene and living conditions had to improve, before medical care could be effective; she travelled to Crimea in South Africa, to attend personally to the wounded soldiers there; she trained the first band of Nightingale nurses, who later travelled to Europe and the US as Matrons helping to train and establish nursing standards in those countries.

Beauty, intellect, charm, wealth, leadership qualities – Florence Nightingale had them all! But the crowning jewel of her personality was her deep sense of care and compassion. In her lifetime, she was able to establish the Florence Nightingale Fund, with which she set up the first School of Nursing in London. She also played a key role in establishing the first Women's Medical College, along with other pioneers.

Few of us know that she was a leading expert in statistics, and had a flair for mathematics too. Her letters, journals and books on Nursing reveal her literary flair and communicative excellence. Above all, she was a committed Christian who followed Jesus's precept to love all human beings: as she herself put it, very simply – "God spoke to me, and called me to His service."

Recently, I met a sister who had participated in a public forum in New Delhi, where members of civil society discussed safety and security issues for women in the National Capital Region (NCR) with representatives from the police and the State and Central Government. This was soon after the terrible incident of molestation and violence that shook the conscience of the entire nation. She told me that at first, the public participants were vociferous with anger and rage at police ineptitude, governmental deficiency and lack of accountability in the state machinery to implement vital security measures. The officials were cornered and literally shouted down by the rising tide of anger and indignation. But suddenly the tide turned. Someone said, in the rising din, that societal apathy was as much to blame as government deficiencies. The girl who had been violently attacked and thrown out to die, had been lying on the road, literally naked and slowly bleeding to death; her companion, who was also badly wounded had appealed to passers-by for help, at least to call the police helpline or emergency number; at least 30-40 cars and two wheelers passed by; NOBODY stopped to help them or even ask them what had happened!

Can there be a more tragic instance of public apathy?

The sister who was part of the forum told me that many shouting men and women were silenced by this statement. Some of them argued that it was fear of police harassment that stopped people from trying to intervene; but this was not a valid argument. The officials pointed out that they need not even have stopped at the spot; they could have gone on further and called the police or even a hospital ambulance service to tell them that there was a fatally injured victim fighting for her life at such and such a place. Alas, no one bothered to make even an anonymous call.

The senior official present then took the offensive stand and asked the people, "What would be your attitude if YOUR sister or daughter was lying there, bleeding to death?"

It is not for us to judge others. But each of us must surely determine to obey the voice of our own conscience in such a situation, must we not? And our conscience would surely say to us: "You are this sister's keeper. Do whatever you can to help her in her distress!"

There is a simple question that all saints ask of us: How can we claim that we love God if we do not love our fellow human beings? How can we call ourselves human beings if we watch our brothers and sisters suffering and struggling?

God is Absolute Love; and if we love God, we must be imbued with the longing to serve our fellow men. I believe that true service is a spiritual activity, which at its best, is born out of the Love of God. It was a true saint of God who said: Prayer without work is as bad as work without prayer!

God cannot be satisfied with our adoration and devotion if they come only from our lips — for words and alphabets cannot make a prayer. It is our hearts and our own lives that must bear witness to our devotion, and what better way to achieve this than through the service of our fellow human beings?

It is possible that some of you may be really overcome by doubts and anxiety when I talk about service to humanity; you may think to yourself, "After all, we are not millionaires. We are people with limited means at our disposal. How can we aspire to serve suffering humanity?"

God can use the least of us in great acts of service, when He so wills. When Jesus fed the five thousand people who had followed him into the hills, he did not use his chief disciples, the apostles as they were called later. In fact, they were full of tension and anxiety, and planning to send the crowds away. Instead, Jesus turned to a small boy whose mother had packed a simple lunch for him. But this boy was willing to give all he had in perfect trust to the Master. I am sure there were many wealthy people in the crowd who had better food with them, but I doubt if they had the faith, trust and devotion of the little boy, who was willing to give his lunch away when the Lord asked him to.

This is the great gift of service – it blesses those who receive and those who serve!

SISTER NIVEDITA

India has reason to feel eternally grateful to some westerners who, when the country was passing through a period of darkness and despair, gave hope and strength to the people. One of them was **Sister Nivedita**, who dedicated the best years of her life to the service of India and her teeming millions. Inspired by Swami Vivekananda's teachings, she dedicated her life to spreading his message. She was a woman of faith and courage, of vision and wisdom. And she urged, if every Indian could spend just ten minutes every evening and remind himself that we all who belong to different races and religions, castes and communities, are children of *Bharat Mata*, India could be one of the greatest nations of the world.

Margaret Elizabeth Noble was a young Irish-Scots girl, who began attending all of Swamiji's lectures in London. Gradually, Swami Vivekananda's teachings penetrated her heart and, as a result, she developed a deep affection for India's ancient culture and heritage.

One day, Swami Vivekananda said to her, "India has need of women like you. At this time, we need people who will help the women-folk of India and try to uplift them. We need to educate them." When Margaret Noble heard those words, she said, "I am ready!"

When she came to live in Calcutta, Swami Vivekananda gave her the name by which she is known all over the world today – Sister Nivedita. She was initiated and made a *brahmacharini*. The meaning of the word "Nivedita" is, "one who has offered herself completely, wholly, to God – the dedicated one". She lived up to her name, in every sense of that term, till the very last breath of her life.

Many and varied were the avenues in which she served Mother India. In the year 1898, she established a school for girls, who were deprived of even basic education. She taught hygiene and healthcare to the people, often taking up a broom to clean filthy streets herself. Her aim was to bring about an improvement in the lives of Indian women belonging to various social classes and castes. She tried to bridge the gap and put an end to the caste distinctions.

Then, all of a sudden, an epidemic of plague struck Calcutta. People panicked. When anyone was struck by plague, even their near and dear ones abandoned them and left the house. At such a time, this English woman went from house to house and offered her services. She would literally knock at their door and ask, "Is there any service required, please let me know. I am ready to serve you." She pleaded with the people, "If you want to stop the spread of plague, then keep the city clean. Keep your homes clean."

One day, she saw some filth in the street. This English woman, who had a special place in her heart for India and the Indians, took up a broom and started sweeping the streets.

When people learnt of this, they came running and said to her, "This work is not for you to do: We are going to do it ourselves." Groups of young men were formed in different parts of the city, who started cleaning the streets of Calcutta. This English lady, by sweeping the streets herself, had set an example to be emulated.

She was respected and admired by many of the day's great intellectuals of the Bengali community such as Rabindranath Tagore, and Jagdish Chandra Bose, the distinguished scientist. She translated several of Tagore's songs into English. It is thought that her book *Kali, the Mother* influenced Abanindranath Tagore, who painted Bharat Mata. She was also an intimate associate and disciple of Ma Sharadamani, whom she loved and revered.

Nivedita was a prolific orator and writer and extensively toured India to deliver lectures, especially on India's culture and religion. Her works included *The Web of Indian Life*, which sought to rectify many myths in the Western world about Indian culture and customs. *The Cradle Tales of Hindusim* is a book that has some of the best renderings in English of the stories from the *Puranas, Ramayana* and *Mahabharata*, Whenever she had the opportunity to converse with Swami Vivekananda, she sat at his feet and took detailed notes of every word he uttered. Many of Swamiji's valuable teachings are with us today, thanks to her diligent note-taking.

She appealed to the Indian youth to work selflessly for the cause of the motherland, and imbued them with the ideals of Swami Vivekananda. Here is what she wrote in one of her editorials in the Journal, *Karma Yogin:*

"The whole history of the world shows that the Indian intellect is second to none. This must be proved by the performance of a task beyond the power of others, the seizing of the first place in the intellectual advance of the world. Is there any inherent weakness that would make it impossible for us to do this? Are the countrymen of Bhaskaracharya and Shankaracharya inferior to the countrymen of Newton and Darwin? We trust not. It is for us, by the power of our thought, to break down the iron walls of opposition that confront us, and to seize and enjoy the intellectual sovereignty of the world."

During the later years of her life, she engaged in activities that promoted the cause of India's Independence. Her writings expressed her pan-Indian nationalist views.

Finally, this great soul left for her heavenly abode on October 13, 1911. Her epitaph reads thus:

"Here reposes Sister Nivedita who gave her all to India".

"What do we live for if not to make the world less difficult for each other?" asks the distinguished writer and novelist, George Eliot. Most of us are inclined to be self-centered and to live narrow, selfish lives; but it is only in selfless living that we can discover the best that we are capable of. And do not restrict 'giving' to the giving of alms, giving money to the poor! You were surely made for higher things – so give of yourself, give of your time, talents and energies to lighten the loads of the weary and the heavy-laden!

And women are rich in love, generosity and the spirit of selfless service! They are always ready to give their loving interest and concern to others – which is worth more than all the money in the world!

"Do you want to be happy? Then make others happy!" was Gurudev Sadhu Vaswani's clarion call to us.

"If you want others to be happy, practise compassion. If you want to be happy, practise compassion," the Dalai Lama tells us.

In loving and compassionate service, in selfless and caring service lies the secret of a peaceful, civilised world community.

"Let everyone who comes to you return to their life feeling better and happier," Mother Teresa would often say to her helpers. If we all tried to follow this simple precept, wouldn't we leave the world a better and happier place?

The true spirit of religion is the spirit of love, sympathy, compassion and selfless service. I think we lack religion in its truest sense if we do not put these virtues into action!

I humbly submit that it is the woman soul that can rekindle the flame of true religion in these dark times. For long have we lived in a male-dominated society with man-made laws that come from the head; what we now require are laws and rules that come from the heart and the spirit. Gurudev Sadhu Vaswani was strongly of the view that the future belongs to women. Today, many men regard themselves as superior to women. But a new civilisation will dawn — a woman-made civilisation, based on the womanly ideals of simplicity, sympathy, service and sacrifice. It is my firm belief that there is a new world in the making – the world of peace, harmony and unity – and of this world the builder would be the woman, not man!

For Your Reflection

The essential distinction between savages and civilised men lies not in differences of dress, dwelling, food, deportment or possessions – but in the way we treat our fellow human beings. It is the degree of humanity in our relationship with others that decides how far we have travelled from a state of savagery towards an ideal world of civilised beings who truly have learnt the art of peaceful co-existence.

– Aung San Suu Kyi

When you express "purity" which is the truth about yourself, you feel a love for yourself that is expressed by self-respect, self-esteem and self-confidence!

- Tae Yun Kim

God has assigned as a duty to every man the dignity of every woman.

- Pope John Paul II

Blessed are the pure in heart, for they shall see God.

- Matthew 5:8

Develop purity, forgiveness, vigour, patience and good will, and avoid pride – these are the riches of the person who is born for heaven.

- Bhagavad Gita

Chapter 13
Purity

I am often asked, "Why is it that we cannot see God?" As human beings, we are unable to see God, because we have not looked within. It is the Law of Nature, that to see God in everything, you first have to experience Him within. Therefore, my humble request to every one of you who wishes to behold God face to face is, try to go within. Let us be in constant quest. We shall surely find Him.

May I tell you a beautiful story I read some time ago?

A small boy once approached his slightly older sister with a question about God. "Didi, can anybody ever really see God?" he asked. Busy with other things, Didi replied curtly, "No, of course not, silly. God is so far up in heaven that nobody can see Him."

Time passed, but his question still lingered. So he approached his mother, "Mama, can anybody ever really see God?"

"No, not really," she said gently. "God is formless and He dwells in our hearts, but we can never really see Him." Somewhat satisfied but still wondering, the youngster went on his way.

Not long afterwards, the little boy went to spend a day with his saintly old grandfather. The old man took the little boy on a walk. They had a great time together – it had been a lovely autumn day. The sun was beginning to set with unusual splendour as the day ended. The old man stopped walking and turned his full attention to the exquisite beauty unfolding before him. On seeing the face of his grandfather reflecting such deep peace and contentment as he gazed into the magnificent ever-changing sunset, the little boy thought for a moment and finally spoke hesitatingly.

"Granddad, I... I... wasn't going to ask anybody else, but I wonder if you can tell me the answer to something I've been wondering since a long time. Can anybody…can anybody ever really see God?"

The old man did not even turn his head. A long moment slipped by before he finally answered.

"My child," he quietly said. "It's getting so dark that I can't see anything else."

It is true God is on a higher plane. But the ascent to that higher plane must be through the ladder of our own inner consciousness! To realise God and see Him, we have to realise our highest level of consciousness. We have to rise above our senses. We have to purify the body and mind. Then the miracle happens. God is visible everywhere. The entire universe is His expression and you can feel it, you can experience it. *Jidhar dekhta hoon, udhar tu hi tu hai!* God then becomes manifest to you. His Higher Energy can be felt everywhere.

Let me tell you of an incident from the life of Gautama Buddha. One day Gautama Buddha was sitting with his devotees. Suddenly, he exclaimed, "Look, look how the flames soar!"

The devotees looked all around. They were perplexed; for there was nothing to look at.

"Look. Look. There is fire everywhere!"

The disciples were confused. Where was the fire that the Master spoke of?

The Buddha said to them, "Every heart is in turmoil; every mind is restless, suffering intense pain – pain that is caused by envy, greed, lust, jealousy, revenge. Man is burning with the fire of desires. Man is consumed by the flames of envy, violence, cruelty and selfish pride. The world is on fire, the heat is soaring, engulfing all humanity in fierce combustion. Even in the midst of the cold winter, man is burning with evil desires."

"Master, how can you say that man can burn in the fire of winter?" asked one of the disciples, innocently. "It is the summer heat that scorches and burns. The winter is kinder and colder."

The Buddha smiled and said, "The fire is within. It may be severely cold outside, with mounds of snow piled up, but inside his heart, man is being consumed by the fire of evil desires. The unbearable heat comes from anger, violence, greed and excessive desire. The fire of *trishna* is enveloping the entire world. Quench the flames of desire, or they will consume you in their fierce heat!"

A Divine life is filled with serenity, purity, peace and joy.

MAA SARADAMANI

Many cultures believe that a woman finds her true identity and greatest fulfillment in the roles of wife and mother. Maa Saradamani was both the splendid example and the brilliant exception to this rule: for she *was* indeed the wife of one of India's dearly beloved saints, Sri Ramakrishna Paramahansa; she was not just the mother of a few children – but rose to become the *sangha mata*, the head of the Ramakrishna order after the death of her husband – and yet she was the devoted disciple as well as the Universal Mother to him! They lived a pure life of celibacy, devoid of all physical contact. Indeed, their marriage was truly the union of two souls. Instead of being dragged down by the burden of worldly living, they elevated themselves to the level of the Divine!

In the vision of the world, she may have been uneducated, unlearned, simple and innocent; but she was an illumined soul. Her life bears witness to the truth that salvation is as open to devoted women, as it is to those who renounce the world and dedicate themselves to a ceaseless search for God.

The most dominant quality of Maa Sarada's life was her motherly love. Her duties as a mother to her congregation were carried out with dignity, sweetness and emotional strength. She was indeed a remarkable saint who combined in herself the role of a devoted mother and a wonderful teacher. She may not have had children of her own – but today, thousands of devotees worship her as the Divine Mother, and the sacred consort of Sri Ramakrishna.

Pure as moonlight, sweet as the gentle breeze, innocent as a lamb, she embodies selfless devotion and serenity of spirit. She was indeed, the incarnation of love, sacrifice, selfless service and purity!

Where are the pure hearts today? Where are the beautiful minds? Purity is missing; so is prayer. Our life is stressed out by vaunting ambition, envy and ugly thoughts. Stress generates heat; high blood pressure and cardiac problems are ample evidence of the heat of stress within us.

Lust is a destructive desire. Lust pushes men into crime. Lust just arises as a desire in the mind. The desire is all consuming – defying all reason. Sensuous desires, if uncontrolled, are harmful – to the self and to the society. These desires gradually become obsessions; they are ruinous and destructive. From the gratification of momentary pleasures, they turn into all-consuming, destructive passions.

I call upon all my brothers and sisters: be alert. Do not entertain such evil desires. Be awake. Do not waste your precious energies in futile pursuits. The flames of lust are terrible! Stay away from lust!

There was a time, in this ancient land of ours, when people lived for others. They had love in their hearts for one another. The spirit of brotherhood was alive amongst them. They were ready to live and die for love; they were ready to sacrifice their lives for love. In India, selfless love flowed like a river. The people lived a very happy and contented life, under the warm shelter of a veritable canopy of love.

Today, in this country, wherever we turn, there is greed for money. All around the country, people fight over religion, people fight for power, they fight for money. It seems they have been blinded by this greed!

People labour under the illusion that money is the greatest power; so they want to earn money by hook or by crook. Money has become the be-all and end-all of their existence.

We live in an excited, agitated world — a world beset with stress and strain. This intensified stress and strain manifests itself physically as heart disease, hypertension and nervous breakdown. Doctors agree that the cause of such ailments is psychological rather than physical. Doctors now agree that it is our stress-prone, restless lifestyle that makes us fall victim to such diseases. The solution, they say, is to alter our lifestyle and find inner equilibrium.

It is not easy to do this – maintain your inner equilibrium at all times and in all situations.

SISTER SHANTI

Even as the most beloved disciple of Krishna was Uddhava; and the dearest disciple of Buddha was Ananda; even so, the most beloved child and disciple of Gurudev Sadhu Vaswani was Shanti. She was but ten years old when she came into contact with him. Soon afterwards, abandoning all ties of kith and kin, she came and dwelt at the feet of the Master. For her, to live was to serve him, to love him, to draw nearer to him, in utter devotion and self-surrender. She surrendered herself in the deepest *Guru bhakti* to him; and in turn, she herself became a picture of love and compassion, with his grace and spiritual influence.

Gurudev Sadhu Vaswani spoke of three stages in the life of a Pilgrim on the path. The first is the stage of the seeker. He sets out in search of someone – a Sage, a saint of God, a *Satpurusha* – who may unravel to him the mystery of his own hidden Self. And having found such a one, he sits at his feet day after day, and imbibes the healing wisdom which flows from the lips and the life of the *Satpurusha*. In this second stage, the seeker becomes a disciple. He walks the way of obedience and devotion and surrender. Then comes the third stage in the spiritual unfoldment of the seeker. He puts into practice the teachings of his Master. He submits himself to a course of discipline. He enters within himself and develops inner powers. And a day comes when the disciple becomes a child of the Master. The disciple becomes like unto the Guru, and beholds the glory that is beyond the words of man to describe.

Under the benign grace of the Master, Shanti reached the third stage. She became a child of the Master. And she, who was originally called Shanti H. Makhijani, was renamed Shanti T. Vaswani.

A number of people wondered how Gurudev Sadhu Vaswani, who was a *bal-brahmachari* (a life-long celibate), could have a daughter. But Shanti's link with Sadhu Vaswani was surely an ancient one.

At the age of twelve, Shanti fell ill. She had an attack of typhoid fever. The fever kept on mounting; it assumed the dangerous form of brain fever. She was given up for lost by her grieving family, when Gurudev Sadhu Vaswani came to see her. He looked at Shanti – her face pallid as death.

"Shanti is about to pass away," they said to him. "It is a question of minutes."

"Do not weep," Gurudev Sadhu Vaswani said to them. "Trust in the Lord."

He went into a room on the top floor of the house and shut himself away in prayer. Hours and hours passed. What is there that the Saints of God cannot do when they commune with the Divine? Downstairs, Shanti's breathing gradually became easier. Her face changed colour. The fever came down. And when Gurudev Sadhu Vaswani came out of the quiet chamber he was told that Shanti's condition had greatly improved. He came and stood by her; and Shanti, who had been unconscious for the past few hours, opened her eyes. She looked at Gurudev Sadhu Vaswani and said to him, "I was at the Kingdom of Krishna, when you came and brought me back to the earth."

And turning to her people she said: "My life on earth was

over. Gurudev Sadhu Vaswani has given me a new lease of life. It no longer belongs to me. It belongs to him. May it be spent in his service!"

Later, when Gurudev Sadhu Vaswani opened an *ashram* at Hyderabad-Sind – an *ashram* for women, where a number of girls received opportunities to grow in the Life of the Spirit, Shanti left her home and went to live at the *Ashram*, close to her Master's lotus feet. She accompanied him wherever he went and sought to bear witness to his teachings in deeds of daily living.

She was a true seeker of perfection. The qualities of such a one are:

1. Equanimity. Whatever happened, she remained calm. Under all circumstances, she was thankful.

2. Acceptance of the Lord's will. She never ever complained about anything.

3. Forgiveness. She easily forgave friend and foe alike.

4. Insight. She realised that what she needed most was the grace of God and the Guru. Worldly wealth had no appeal for her.

5. Humility. She was humble as ashes and dust.

6. Purity. In thought and word and deed, she remained ever pure, dedicating her life as an offering to God and the Guru.

Her life was an offering at the feet of her beloved Master, in the service of the poor and the needy. She was also deeply involved in the cause of alleviating the cruelty done to birds and animals. To everyone whose lives she had touched, she was verily a gift from God.

If I were asked to give a summing up of dear Shanti's life in a few simple words, I would say: "She loved God with all her mind and heart and soul, and she gave the service of love to all who came to her in need – the poor and broken ones, the forsaken and forlorn, and brother birds and animals." Hers was a truly dedicated life!

Sister Shanti was one who spoke the language of the heart – one whose sensitive intuitions and emotions made her a living example of absolute faith and acceptance.

Gurudev Sadhu Vaswani dropped his physical body on January 16, 1966. To Shanti, life on earth, without Gurudev, had little meaning or value. She longed for the day, when, passing through the portals of death she would be back with her Master. The call came to her on the night of May 15, 1970. A soft smile played upon her serene face. She welcomed death as an intimate friend. "Death unites us with the Beloved," she said, "in an everlasting bond. Death is the gateway to the Life Immortal!"

Shanti was a true child of the Spirit. Her heart was a temple in which there was room only for the Lord. Again and again, she retired into the temple – the temple of the Heart – and adored the One Beloved, forgetting all else. Then she came out – her face radiant with the light of Eternity – and served the poor and the needy, served birds and animals. Her life was a poem of purity, a song of sacrifice, a lamp of service. Hers was a truly dedicated life, for while engaged in the common tasks of life, she was absorbed in the song of the soul within – the song of the Lord.

There are many people who believe that peace and inner equilibrium can be found up in the Himalayas! I know many brothers and sisters who believe that frequent trips to Leh-Ladakh and the snow-capped Himalayas can give them lasting peace. And for this they trek miles and miles in search of the elusive thing called peace – inside mountain caves and unchartered valleys and in the dense forests. It is true that they experience peace for a while; but such experiences are too short lived. What these people fail to realise is that peace is not external; it cannot be derived from the external environment. Peace is an inner thing. It comes from our own inner environment.

There are people who take to pilgrimages; they travel to Kashi and Mathura, they take dips in the holy rivers, they participate in the Kumbh Mela and seek that elusive thing called peace.

It is certainly good that we go on pilgrimages. But are we aware of the baggage we carry with us on these sacred trips? I do not mean your hand baggage or checked in baggage; I mean your mental baggage. When a man goes to these places of worship what does he carry with him? His inner self is filled with desires. His mind is filled with negative emotions. Sadly enough, man thinks and believes that these negative emotions are externally induced. He puts the blame of his 'anger' on someone who has irritated him. If a lustful thought arises in his mind, he thinks it is caused by the presence of women.

There are basically five evils of mind: Anger, Greed, Lust, Attachment and Ego. These five evil desires control our life. We need to be freed from the clutches of these negativities! We need to be cleansed internally!

How can we hope to have a vision of God when our inner world is so dark? Our inner self is impure; it is polluted, and we have to cleanse it. If only we could create a sacred place for Him, He will surely come and sit in the Lotus of our hearts. Even animals search for a clean space to sit. Have you observed a dog? It cleans the place with its bushy tail and then sits there. Even a dog loves cleanliness! Imagine how much more must God love cleanliness. Cleanse yourself! Cleanse your interior self.

We often put several restrictions on devotees to keep our places of worship clean. No alcohol! No smoking! No non-vegetarian food! Kindly wash your feet before you enter. Leave your footwear outside. Why do we insist on these injunctions? We want our places of worship to be clean.

May I ask you: what about cleansing the inner self? What are we going to do about the thousand impurities that we carry within?

We drink alcohol, we smoke, we speak lies, we harbour negative emotions and we carry evil desires within and then say why don't I see God?

I said to you earlier that many of us remain trapped in the entanglements of the world. This is true of every *sansari jeev* – he is intoxicated with the pleasures, possessions and powers of this world. He is intoxicated with worldly love and longing – for I, Me and Mine.

He must detoxify himself of this *maya* and enter into another kind of intoxication – he must lose himself, nay, drown himself in the intoxication of God's love. Such a one will find himself shedding unbidden tears of love and longing for the true and only Beloved.

First and foremost to be conquered must be the desire for sense-gratification: this is what Sri Ramakrishna referred to when he spoke of *'Kamini'*, the personification of sense-indulgence, as one whom we must guard against.

We are told that the devil once called for a meeting of all its associates. It was a stock-taking session to determine which of them could wrack the greatest havoc on mankind.

Anger, jealousy, greed and envy were present, among others. Each one boasted of his numerous victims. Soon, a heated argument ensued; who, among them, could cause the most damage?

Impurity won, hands down. Conferring the dubious distinction upon him, the devil remarked, "He is the one with the sharpest sword, the deadliest weapon. All he has to do is to sow a single thought of impurity in the mind – and that will take care of the rest."

When lust, desire, greed and craving dominate our minds, how can we embark upon any spiritual practice?

A sociologist from the US rues the fact that today, there are very few places where young people can be safe from indecently suggestive sensual temptations; even supermarket shelves are loaded with books, magazines and videos, whose covers no decent publication would have carried twenty years ago! Children cannot be permitted to run around unsupervised; television has become a parental nightmare; even radio stations relay songs that can shock people born thirty years ago! As for the home computer which has now morphed into the hand held tablet, it is loaded with content that no child should ever set eyes on!

The Arabic word for woman is *hurmah*, which means 'what is sacred'. Purity and chastity are a good woman's natural virtues, and it is from women that men must learn them. Unfortunately, even as woman's spiritual strength is effulgent, so is her physical attraction to men. It is this attraction that makes men lose self control and turn to aggression, violence and molestation. I am not suggesting that women are responsible for these vile transgressions! I only urge them to be spiritually strong so that their inner purity may give them the power to protect themselves from harm. In respecting and elevating women, we respect and elevate ourselves; in abusing or degrading them, we degrade ourselves!

I have said to you that simplicity, sympathy, selfless service and purity are the special qualities of women; when men imbibe these qualities, they get close to the Divine; when these qualities are totally absent in men, they become no better than beasts! To quote the words of Chanakya, "Purity of speech, of the mind, of the senses, and of the compassionate heart is needed by one who desires to rise to the level of the Divine."

The saint-poet Thiruvalluvar asks us: What greater treasure can there be, than a woman who has the abiding strength of purity? This 'purity' according to scholars is much, much more than chastity or celibacy; it is an 'abiding moral tenacity' to never ever let evil enter her heart. Such a woman brings the triple blessing of virtue, wealth and happiness to her family. Nor does this ancient treatise recommend that women be confined to a restricted life to protect her purity. The poet asks boldly: "Of what avail is close confinement? It is women's own discipline that is the best guardian of their virtue."

Much of what I have said to you regarding purity is not likely to be acceptable to the 'free' thinkers of today. We are now beginning to uphold the qualities of 'tolerance' and 'understanding' for sexual and moral transgressions. I have heard arguments that sex is beautiful and that it should have no strings attached to it; I have also heard people insist that God made men and women for the sole purpose of enjoying each other 'in the flesh' and that any idea of attaching guilt and sin and shame to a sexual relationship outside marriage is indecent and bigoted.

I beg to differ. Perhaps the severe restrictions placed on men and women are now having a contrary effect and pulling them in a reverse direction that can only be to their own detriment. Everybody chooses their own moral standards, their own values and ideals to live by; but I have no right to drag others' values and moral principles down to justify my own immoral preferences!

Why is virtue resented by many people today? First, living the virtuous life is not easy. It requires a lot of effort, practice and self-denial. We are constantly battling against our fallen, selfish human nature. On this side of the Garden of Eden, it is a lot easier to give in to our emotions and desires than it is to control them. For example, it is easier to indulge in our appetite than it is to eat with moderation. It is easier to loose our temper when things don't go our way than it is to moderate our anger. It is easier to give in to discouragement and complaining than it is to joyfully endure our trials with courage.

The virtue that is probably resented the most today is chastity. Chastity is no longer seen as something good, something noble, something we should all pursue. Just the opposite: Chastity is now often portrayed as something evil - something harmful for human beings!

Some argue that chastity is harmful to the psychological well-being of young men and women. Sexual desire is natural, it is said. Therefore, it is unnatural to restrict it in any way.

– Courtesy: Belief net

For Your Reflection

This is why some people resent the virtues. Instead of being inspired to live a better life, they destroy the moral standard of the virtues and drag it down to their level. In other words, they minimise the significance of virtues in order to spare themselves the effort and excuse their own moral failures.

– Dr. Edward P. Sri

Whatever you do, make it an offering to Me - the food you eat, the sacrifices you make, the help you give; even your suffering.

- Sri Krishna in the Bhagavad Gita

Sacrifice, which is the passion of great souls, has never been the law of societies.

- Henri Frederic Amiel

I have worshipped woman as the living embodiment of the spirit of service and sacrifice.

- Mahatma Gandhi

This was what love meant after all - sacrifice and selflessness. It did not mean hearts and flowers and a happy ending, but the knowledge that another's well-being is more important than one's own.

- Melissa de la Cruz

Chapter 14
Sacrifice: Priority By Choice

In the days of yore, 'sacrifice' had an altogether different connotation from the term as we are using it here; it actually referred to ritual slaughter, that is, an act of slaughtering an animal or person or surrendering a possession as an offering to God or to a Divine or supernatural figure.

Gurudev Sadhu Vaswani often said to us that we are not called upon to sacrifice sheep or goats or hens for the sake of ritual *yajnas;* what we really need to give up as 'offerings', he pointed out, are the animals within us: the dragon of anger and revenge; the ferocious beast of hatred and jealousy; the demons of greed and lust. This meant giving up our lower *vaasanas* and entering a higher plane of consciousness.

I use the word sacrifice in its more symbolic sense here, which is to forfeit or renounce something of value to oneself, for the sake of a larger, more valuable claim. Thus many large-hearted men and women 'give up' their precious time, efforts and even money to contribute their mite to a cherished cause. Many volunteers working for Red Cross or Oxfam, leave the comforts of their homes in highly developed countries to live and work among less privileged people in Africa or Asia. The Latin root of the word sacrifice actually means "to make holy" or "to make sacred". In this sense, the religious denotation persists. The person who willingly and lovingly forfeits or gives up something valuable thereby makes that offering sacred in the eyes of the Lord.

The ideal of selfless sacrifice has always been held high at our Sadhu Vaswani Mission. Our Founder himself was the supreme example of selfless living and sacrificial renunciation. A deeply spiritual young man, he set aside his profound spiritual aspirations to make his mother's wishes come true. He took up an academic career and rose to become the Principal of several prestigious colleges across Punjab and Sind provinces, making his mother proud and fulfilling her dearest dreams to see her son well placed in life. But the moment she passed away, he resigned his job and set out to seek the truth of life as a *fakir,* an ascetic, living a life of frugality far removed from the comforts of a Principal's position. In his case, worldly life and a successful professional career were in itself a sacrifice of a very high order. But he did it out of love for his mother, and did not regret it!

The point I wish to make is this: the notion of sacrifice, like the quality of mercy, cannot be strained; it has to be instinctive, spontaneous, not forced or laboured. And the example that comes naturally to mind is motherhood. Nobody tells a mother that she has to lose out on her sleep or her pastimes, restrict her diet or give up her leisure hours or her favourite outings when her little baby is growing up. But most young mothers do it all anyway!

MOTHER TERESA

It was Jesus Christ who said, "Whatever you do to the least of the little ones, that you verily do unto me!"

Mother Teresa did exactly that – she served the homeless, the destitute, the dying, the forsaken and forlorn, the unwanted and unloved ones who had been abandoned by their own people and the rest of humanity; she served them with love and devotion making selfless service the goal of her life. She gathered to her heart those from whom the world turned away in proud disdain. She came to be known as "The saint of the gutters".

A white European born in Macedonia, she chose to make India her *Karma bhumi* – the plane of her action and dedication. Posted to begin her life as an ordained nun in Calcutta, once described as a "dying city", she became the guardian angel, the spiritual support to the poor, the old, the dying and the disease-stricken people of the city.

A French journalist who came to visit Calcutta and was tremendously moved by her work, bestowed a new name on the chaotic, teeming city of the Communists – Calcutta became "The City of Joy", blessed by Mother Teresa's benevolent presence.

Mother Teresa's mission of help and healing was not carried out in the aseptic environs of a state-of-the-art-hospital. She dedicated her life's work to the slum dwellers who lived in filthy, foul-smelling areas, and were victims of several diseases. Her service was not publicized through "success" stories of the people whose lives she had saved; rather, it was to her credit that she enabled the dying destitutes to live the last days of their lives peacefully, and die with grace and dignity.

India's own Bharat Ratna – the Jewel of India – she remarked when she accepted the Nobel Peace Prize, that her life's mission was "to care for the hungry, the naked, the homeless, the crippled, the blind, the lepers, and all those who feel unwanted...people who have become a burden to the society and are shunned by everyone..."

Is it not significant that we will always remember the Blessed Theresa of Calcutta by the name of "The Mother"!

The other day, we were discussing these special qualities of women, when a sister said to me, somewhat sharply, "Dada, I distrust this word sacrifice. A woman writer whom I admire, says, 'Where there's sacrifice, there's someone collecting the sacrificial offerings. Where there's service, there is someone being served.' The point she makes is this: when anyone talks to you of sacrifice and service, they are really referring to slaves and masters, and they mean that someone intends to be your master. Tell me Dada, are we supposed to sacrifice what is dear to us, just to uphold male superiority and male mastery and domination?"

I said to her gently, "In such a case it would be coercion or compulsion; it would not be called sacrifice. But I do concede your point: in the family, it is the women, the mothers, sisters and daughters who readily come forward to put others' interests before their own. Although, honesty compels me to add that many fathers and sons too, can be selfless in their caring and loving protection of the family."

I think that the very term 'sacrifice' may have negative, distasteful associations for the younger generation; but I know many young people, most of them students or young graduates about to enter their first jobs, who often tell me that they have voluntarily given up movies or parties or TV serials or novels or other such pastimes in order to focus their attention and efforts on the one highly desired goal that they have chosen for themselves: passing the examinations with a First Class or clearing a Job interview/Selection process to enter a good company. They are willing to give up something that they enjoy, something that is pleasurable, something that is dear to them for the sake of a greater good.

In the past, mothers stayed home to take care of their children as a matter of course. It would not have occurred to them that they were 'sacrificing' anything to fulfill the duties of motherhood. But today, many women feel that they have to 'sacrifice' their careers and their professional ambitions in order to become mothers. Equally, there are others too, who find it easy to turn their back on lucrative careers and professions to embrace the joys of being a wife, mother and homemaker. For them, there is no question of 'sacrificing' anything. It is their choice after all!

If we are to reexamine our terminology, perhaps we should use instead of sacrifice, the phrase 're-examining one's priorities'. Each of us has to make choices at every turn of life. Poor youngsters in rural areas are often forced to go out to work in order to support their families. Some rich boys and girls resent having to attend classes in school or college, while their less fortunate peers yearn to be well educated and make something of their lives. Many young men are working night shifts in stressful work situations, while their peers are out pursuing youthful larks. If a young woman is forced to leave her children at home (with or without proper guardians to care for them) and constrained to earn a livelihood, is she under compulsion or is she sacrificing her preferences for her family? If a mother of two growing children decides that she needs to devote her time and attention to them and chooses to give up her job, is she sacrificing her career for her children?

When a decision that involves a difficult personal choice is made out of love, there is no question of compulsion or coercion; the person who takes that decision would hardly deem it a sacrifice that she is making for those who love!

Let me make one thing very clear. Men are as capable of selfless sacrifices as women are: they go into their work or business almost without giving it a thought that they are doing what they have to for the sake of their family. The security of the family, the future of their children is of paramount importance to them.

Many sisters tell me that their domestic help, the *bais* or servant maids who report for work daily, have very similar stories to share. More often than not, their husbands are unemployed; or if they are actually working and earning a salary, they do not bother to hand it to their wives or make any effort to buy food and groceries for the family. Some of them even drink or gamble away all their earnings. These *bais* take on tough domestic chores just to feed their children and keep the household going. They can stay at home and fight with their husbands; they can even walk out of their homes; but they stick on, many of them uncomplaining, and some of them making the best of their bad situations. They will laugh at you if you tell them that they are sacrificing their lives for the family; for them it's all literally a day's work!

Soldiers leave their loved ones and their families behind and risk their lives to protect our borders. And when called upon, they are ready to make the supreme sacrifice and lay down their lives for their country.

Therefore, this would be my answer to the young lady who objected to the word 'sacrifice'. Where there is love, it is just an offering of the heart; where love is missing, it can only be compulsion or coercion. This is why our mothers and grandmothers would laugh at us if we question them on the sacrifices they made for the family; they did it out of love. I dare say that they would do it all over again if they had to.

Making offerings out of love and prioritising one's choices to protect the interests of the loved ones comes easily to women – call it sacrifice or whatever else you will!

KASTURBA GANDHI

All of us hail Mahatma Gandhi as the Father of the nation. Most of us know several details about his life. But not enough is known or recognised about the life and activities of the woman who stood behind him, by his side, and offered invaluable moral support to him throughout his life. Kasturba Gandhi, the wife of the Mahatma, is not much discussed these days; her life is not studied by many. But we will do well to remember that Gandhiji said of her in his autobiography, that he learnt the very basics of *satyagraha* and non-violence from his wife. She was never aggressive or strident; but she was not a passive and silent sufferer either; she was someone who stood up for what she believed was right; and more importantly, she was willing to change her mind when she was convinced of the truth of what she saw and heard. From a practically illiterate child bride, she evolved to become a woman of spiritual strength, fortitude and patriotism, whose presence by Mahatma Gandhiji's side, drew thousands of women to join the Freedom Movement. Indeed, she played a silent but predominant role in the transformation of the young man called Mohandas Karamchand Gandhi into Mahatma Gandhi, the Father of the Nation.

Born in 1869, Kasturba was the daughter of a prosperous businessman from a conservative family. According to the customs of those times, she was given away in marriage to the son of the Dewan of Porbandar, when she was just 13 years old. Nowadays, we know that child marriages are illegal and we regard them as uncivilised and regressive. But many of our grandmothers and great grandmothers were child brides in their days and we must understand the logic behind this practice. Their families feared for the safety of their young girls in the unmarried state; and the thinking was that if girls were sent to live with their husband's families as children, they would grow into the customs and traditions of the family without facing problems of adjustment or emotional differences. Whatever the reasons for her early marriage, records tell us that Kasturba was practically illiterate when she married Gandhiji. Both the bride and the bridegroom were of the same age, 13; and one of the first things that Gandhiji 'imposed' on her was to learn to read and write.

When the Gandhi family fell on difficult times with the passing away of the father, it was decided that young Mohandas should be sent to England to train as a barrister; we are told that Kasturba's jewels were pawned to pay for his education abroad. Thus Kasturba's sacrifices began very early in life. From now on she had to suffer long periods of separation from her husband; she was already the mother of a son and she virtually had to bring up her four sons single handedly. She acutely felt the absence of their father's presence on her sons and even felt aggrieved about it; but she could not do anything to mend matters. The conservative community to which she belonged, practically excommunicated her husband because he dared to 'cross the seas' which was then forbidden. This was a terrible thing for the traditional-minded Kasturba to bear; but she took it all, suffering internally, and yet supporting her husband and his family.

After prolonged separation, Kasturba was finally able to set up a home with her husband and her sons, when she accompanied Gandhi to South Africa, where they lived for more than 19 years. But this was certainly not a time of idyllic domestic bliss and harmony for Ba. Gandhiji was a harsh taskmaster when it came to imposing his principles on his wife; tasks like cleaning the toilets, cooking and eating with Christians and Muslims, even such a simple thing like wearing shoes inside the house – these were strange and frightening practices for the young wife and mother. But she took it all, in patience and fortitude, and came to see the truth and justice of her husband's beliefs. She was sent to prison in South Africa, under harsh conditions of hard labour; but she unconsciously took on the leadership role among women, who came to look upon her as their leader and role-model.

It was here in South Africa that Gandhiji took on the vow of celibacy. He has stated that it was his wife's support that enabled him to become a strict practitioner of *brahmacharya*.

When Gandhiji returned to India in 1915, Kasturba was his chief assistant in setting up the Sabarmati *ashram*. She was also his able partner in promoting the *khadi* (handspun cloth) movement, and organised its propaganda. She fasted with her husband whenever he took up his protest fasts. His goal became her ideal, and she was always his silent and strong supporter. She travelled with him far and wide; when he conferred with the men on the politics of the freedom struggle, she went among the women and spoke to them of basic hygiene and childcare. He was sacrificing his life for the country; she was his partner in suffering and sacrificed her life for his ideals.

Ba gave exemplary leadership to women's participation in the *Satyagraha* Movement. But the constant fasting and frequent jail terms affected her health severely. When they were imprisoned together and lodged at the Aga Khan Palace in Yerawada, Pune, she became fatally ill. Kasturba Gandhi died in her husband's arms on February 22, 1944.

Gandhiji was shattered by the death of Ba with whom he had shared more than sixty years of life together. He grieved, "I can't imagine a life without Ba. She has gone away to her freedom, imprinting on her heart, the ideal *to do or die*."

Gandhiji, whom we regard as the apostle of *ahimsa* (non-violence) and *satyagraha* (non-violent resistance) admitted more than once that he learned the art and science of *satyagraha* from his wife. She worked with him and supported him in all the great transformations of his life. He felt that her life was an extremely sacred one. She sacrificed her all, in supporting his principles and ideals.

It is my opinion that child bearing, giving birth, nurturing and mothering are not just biological functions given to a woman. I am convinced that there is something special in their mental, emotional and psychological make up that renders them fit for these special functions. It may be true that in a dark, ignorant age, these were thought to be weaknesses, even severe limitations placed on women, and they were therefore regarded as being inferior. But that kind of ignorance is not accepted in thinking societies. Women's mothering, nurturing functions are recognised and given due weightage in terms of maternity leave and flexitime and working from home. At least the more enlightened companies allow them sufficient breaks to raise their children and welcome them back to the working fold when they are free to join.

Nevertheless, I still persist in my belief that women make those loving sacrifices that bring joy and harmony to marriage and family life. All over the world, it is the woman who uproots herself from her home and family to join the husband in his home when she marries. Apart from nineteenth century examples like that of Prince Albert who condescended to marry Queen Victoria and become her 'consort', there are few men who leave everything behind to go and live with their wives!

I do not like to think of such matters as a 'compromise' made by women. What is compromise in love and marriage? It is not a bargain or a transaction that one can think of give and take or pros and cons. That is why a woman's role is so important in making a marriage successful! She does everything with love; she sees her priorities with a clear eyed perception that comes from the heart.

I would like to share with you what I feel is true renunciation, true sacrifice. It is the offering of the ego, of the pride or *ahankara*. Our scriptures and our saints do not tell us to renounce the world; what they ask of us is to give up the pride in "I" and "mine". I think this is easier for women to achieve!

What is the way of love? The way of love is selflessness. It is the way of sacrifice. Love has no place for ego or selfishness. Love is an ever expanding positive energy. It was Rabindranath Tagore who said, "Love is an endless mystery, for it has nothing else to explain it." I cannot define or explain love to you! You have to feel it in your heart; you have to experience its healing, purifying powers, for it blesses both those who love, and those who are loved. Even such a blessing do women confer on those whom they love.

Every Mother lives her life for another. Those of you who have been mothers - for the love of your child, you have been through the excruciating pain of labour. For the love of your child, you had your sleep disturbed as you wake to feed your baby and change his or her nappy. For the love of your child, you have massively reduced your social life - think how much more you used to go out before you had your child than you did when your child was young. For the love of your child, you structured your entire day around things like school drop off and school pick up times. And on top of all the practical things you did for your child, you spent your time constantly thinking about what would be best for her or him. Every mother lives her life for another.

Our mothers are an inspiration to the rest of us. Every mother exists not for her own benefit but for the benefit of her children. We too, need to learn more and more to exist not for our own benefit but for the benefit of others.

– Rev. Thompson

For Your Reflection

An irate citizen wrote the following words in an angry letter to the headmistress and teachers of his local school in Connecticut, who were vehemently opposing the city's plan to close down the school music class and library.

"You, as a public sector employee, don't generate any revenue. Every penny of the budget of your public-sector enterprise is taken from producers. It's other people's money versus money your organisation earned. Your salary is not market-based. Neither your salary nor your benefits, nor your job is in jeopardy during contracting economic times. If I want a raise I have to prove I have contributed more to the bottom line, and then it doesn't matter unless the entire firm has grown the bottom line sufficiently to give me that raise. You are insulated from that reality. ... How is that fair? Especially in light of the fact that you don't even generate the revenue that pays for your constantly rising salary?"

The week after that letter was written, six educators from the school died, while trying to protect the 6 and 7-year-old students in their care from a psychopath killer's semi-automatic weapon. They were classroom teachers, a school psychologist, a behavioural therapist and a principal.

And they are heroes.

According to police officials, Dawn Hochsprung, the popular principal, was shot lunging at the killer's weapon. Mary Sherlach, school psychologist, was shot when she dashed into a hallway to warn children and other adults.

First-grade teacher Victoria Soto died by sheltering her students in a classroom closet, coming between them and the gunman. Anne Marie Murphy, a special-education teacher, was killed while placing her body in front of a rain of bullets to protect her charges.

Rachel D'Avino was shot shielding her students. Substitute teacher Lauren Rousseau was shot before she could react to the gunman.

Teachers and other staff members who survived the rampage saved children's lives. How many other civilian jobs do we have in which we are expected to give our lives for those in our care?

How about the teacher-bashing state legislators, members of Congress and governors? How many would use their bodies to shield others from a mad gunman?

What about business owners who are raking in millions of dollars from the school privatisation movement? Would they put their lives on the line for school children?

– Bill Maxwell, for the *Ventura County Star*

As you smell the fragrance of a flower by handing it or the smell of sandalwood by rubbing it against a stone, so you obtain spiritual awakening by constantly thinking of God.

- Sri Sarada Devi

Accustom yourself continually to make many acts of love, for they enkindle and melt the soul.

- Saint Teresa of Avila

The soul should always stand ajar, ready to welcome the ecstatic experience.

- Emily Dickinson

Tenderness and kindness are not signs of weakness and despair, but manifestations of strength and resolution.

- Khalil Gibran

Chapter 15
Mindful Spirituality

A s I said to you earlier, women have always been regarded as the custodians of *dharma*, the transmitters of culture and tradition in this ancient land of ours. Therefore, is it said in our scriptures: *yatra naryastu pujyante ramante tatra devatah.* Where women are respected, there the Gods dwell.

Most of us do not realise that this is also the saying of one of our ancient lawgivers. If we hear it mentioned, we are content to just pay lip service to it and let it pass. We do not ask ourselves, "Are we really giving due respect to the women in our life? Do we look upon other women as sisters and mothers and daughters?"

And why do we have to respect and revere women? Whether she chooses to take on the role of the mother or the wife in the *grihast ashrama*, or enters *vaanaprastha* with her life partner, or elects to live the life of a *brahmacharini;* a woman brings with her those special qualities of *ahimsa,* tolerance, understanding, kindness and compassion, which are the foundation of a spiritual life.

Women seem to have played a very conservative and fundamental role in the evolution of society. As distinguished anthropologist, Richard Leakey, points out, the mother-child relationship "is the social unit out of which all higher orders of society are constructed." Without children, a culture cannot survive, and through the millennia, the mother-child dyad has been a fixed and protected center point around which culture has developed.

All her life, a woman loves, gives, serves… For selflessness comes easily to her, as does spiritual aspiration.

Elisabeth Debold, a feminist scholar, remarks with her tongue firmly-in-cheek: "Western culture still suffers from male bias — from Our Father in Heaven and the occupants of the Oval Office to the ravaging of Mother Nature and the ever-intensifying sexual objectification of women (and girls). The recipe for cultural change has been pretty much 'add women and stir'— as if reaching some balance in the numbers of men and women in public life, which has not even happened, would transform the basic ethos of our culture and shift the course of history."

But even the most disillusioned of feminists agree that there is a perceptible change now: there is a definite attempt to create a new spiritual and ethical environment which would balance (or even cancel out) the overbearing male energies of violence, aggression and power-seeking with a turning towards the sacralisation of the feminine. The "Divine Feminine" has been perceived by different people in different ways; many see it in the life-giving, life-sustaining, life-nourishing roles of motherhood; others speak of the intense feminine soul-energy that is creative, imaginative and emotionally powerful; the worship of the Divine Feminine has also made a powerful revival…It is clearly being recognised that women will be the harbingers of the new age of spirituality.

JULIAN OF NORWICH

Have you been inspired, uplifted by the well known saying, ""All shall be well, and all manner of things shall be well"? Have you thrilled to the words of assurance: "God loved us before he made us; and his love has never diminished and never shall."

The lady who wrote these beautiful words was Dame Julian of Norwich. She was an English anchoress (i.e. one who retires from society for religious reasons) who is regarded as one of the leading Christian mystics of all times. The Lutheran and Anglican churches venerate her, but she has not been canonized by the Roman Catholic Church whose faith she followed.

She is thought to have lived between 1342 and 1416. This was a terrible period in English history. It was the time of the Black Death or plague which led to very bad social conditions and the oppression of the poor. As her biographer tells us: "There was a shortage of labour, high taxes and bad harvests, prices were soaring and unrest was bound to follow. The climax of this unrest was the Peasants Revolt in 1381. The wider Church was also in a sorry state: the Religious Orders were at loggerheads, the Papacy had left Rome and was in exile at Avignon in France, and not half a mile from Dame Julian's Church, the early followers of the Protestant John Wycliff, The Lollards, were being burnt in the Lollards Pit, just the other side of the river. It is into this dire situation that the lady we know as Julian of Norwich who calls herself a simple, unlettered creature, comes bringing with her a message of divine love and hope."

The fact is that we know very little of her life. All we know from her writings is that at the age of 30, she was afflicted with a severe illness, and came to believe that she was on her deathbed. She now had a series of intense visions of Jesus Christ which changed her life forever.

She was at home during this near-death experience, and we know nothing of her life prior to this event. These visions brought her great peace and joy. She became an anchoress or hermit, living in a small hut near the church in Norwich, where she devoted the rest of her life to prayer and contemplation of the meaning of her visions.

She wrote down all the details of this blessed vision in what is now known as *A Short Text*. Nearly thirty years later, she wrote an interpretation of the same visions in what is called *A Long Text*. This led to her major work in English, which is called *Sixteen Revelations of Divine Love*. It is dated around 1393 AD. It is an outstanding work in terms of its clarity and depth of vision and its tremendous spiritual intensity.

Whatever her family circumstances, we can conclude that she had sufficient education to become the first woman known to have written a book in English, *Sixteen Revelations of Divine Love*.

Here is a passage from her writing, rendered in modern English:

Thus I was taught that love was our Lord's meaning. And I saw quite clearly in this and in all, that before God made us, he loved us, which love was never slaked nor ever shall be. And in this love he has done all his work, and in this love he has made all things profitable to us. And in this love our life is everlasting. In our creation we had a beginning. But the love wherein he made us was in him with no beginning. And all this shall be seen in God without end ...

Julian encourages us to keep on praying, to keep on thanking, trusting, rejoicing – in God and others knowing that life is not absurd but has a divine purpose.

The precise date of her death is uncertain. Julian is honored with a feast day on May 13 in the Roman Catholic tradition and on May 8 in the Anglican and Lutheran traditions.

In the simplest terms, spirituality is the aspiration, the genuine effort to know our true self. As I said earlier, it begins with the realisation that we are not the bodies we wear; that this materialistic world we live in, cannot satisfy our deepest aspirations; that our unquenchable desire for wealth and power cannot really give us the joy and peace that we truly crave...

Finding your soul – that is the essence of spirituality. And as women attempt to rediscover, reassert their true identity, they emphasise the spiritual dimension that is unique to them.

And today, as more and more women are beginning to debate solutions to the problems of rape and violence and molestation, many of them are in their own diverse ways, beginning to arrive at one distinct conclusion: the answer to mindless violence must lie in *mindful* spirituality. There has to be a definite attempt to infuse spirituality in males from a very early age, perhaps by relooking and even revamping our traditional 'moral instruction' or 'value education' courses at school and college level.

Spirituality is a value; it is an attitude towards life; an approach to the purpose of existence. All of us subsist on a physical plane; we cannot do without those basic needs – *roti, kapda aur makaan* as they are called – food, clothing and shelter. However, all of us have desires that go beyond these needs; we crave for more wealth, more possessions, more acquisitions; but the intelligent ones among us know that wealth and possessions cannot really make us happy. We live by our passions; beyond what we crave passionately, we live by our own sets of morals and values; we look to higher ideals; we are fascinated by the rare moments in our life when we are filled with awe, wonder and a sense of mystery... feelings, moods, aspirations that send our spirits soaring...

Women know, more clearly than men do, that none of these finer feelings can be captured by a materialistic way of life!

In the past, the distinction between spirituality and the workaday world was so sharp that people turned their back on one to face the other squarely. They renounced the world and worldly activities to contemplate on the higher things of life. But today, the boundaries have softened.

What I mean about the blurring of boundaries is that all of us, laymen and women, students and working professionals, businessmen and managers, young and old are deeply concerned about our holistic growth as human beings. Everybody is concerned about their inner life; everyone craves for a sense of peace and harmony that is central to their being. We may not want to renounce the world to find that elusive peace; but we are ready and willing to spend some time focussing our attention on the rich interior world that is within us.

Modern genetics emphasises the concept of human uniqueness. Our genetic inheritance ensures that certain attributes have been passed on to us from our parents. Some of us are tall, like our fathers; some of us are fair, like our mothers. Some of us inherit the sharp wit and sharper tongue of our grandmothers! But we have a far more valuable inheritance that sets us apart from animals – our cultural and spiritual inheritance. We belong to a great culture with a rich legacy of literature, art, religion and philosophy – a valuable legacy that must be preserved, protected, indeed enhanced, to be passed on to generations after our own. We are not only passing on our hereditary biological system to our children; we are passing on the cultural inheritance and spiritual ideals which go back to the Vedas! This is the great responsibility of the mother, the wife and the women of each and every family!

The *rishis* of ancient India have taught us that there are three kinds, three levels of energy: *bahubalam* or physical energy; *buddhibalam* or intellectual energy, *atmabalam* or spiritual energy, which is truly tremendous and beyond compare! This is what our women, our mothers and grandmothers, aunts and sisters can pass on to the younger generations!

ANANDAMAYI MA

On April 30, 1896 in the sleepy and peaceful village of Kheora, in the district of Tripura, which is now in Bangladesh, a girl child was born to Bipin Bihari Bhattacharya and Mokshada Sundari Devi. The child was named Nirmala Sundari (meaning immaculate beauty), for she was indeed a captivating child. The couple were devout Hindus. They had lost a daughter born earlier; and so Mokshada would take the newborn infant and roll her over and over on the ground in front of the Tulsi sapling in the courtyard. She continued to do this for the first eighteen months of the child's life.

Nirmala had barely a few years of education, before she was betrothed to a suitable young boy, Ramani Mohan Chakravarthy, also known as Bholanath. When she went to live with him five years later, Nirmala performed all the duties expected of a young Hindu wife meticulously. The young couple lived for some time with Ramani Mohan's eldest brother. During this period, Nirmala cheerfully took up most of the household chores like cooking, cleaning, fetching water, taking care of the children, etc. as her elder sister-in-law was often indisposed. And she was always a kind, cheerful, good-humored girl, ever willing to help others.

At the age of 18, when she and her husband moved to Bajitpur, she began to undertake *sadhanas* including yogic postures and *mantra* incantations, which came to her of their own accord, without initiation or formal training at the feet of a guru. She often remained in meditation throughout the day. Referring to this period of her life, Sri Ma has said, "*Sadhanas* by which man endeavors to attain self-realisation are of endless variety, and each variety has innumerable aspects. All these simply revealed themselves to me as a part of myself."

Like Sri Ramana Maharishi and other saints, Ma did not receive a formal initiation from any Guru; one day, she initiated herself, and soon after this, her husband was the first to be initiated by her. From then on, their relationship was that of the guru and disciple.

It must be mentioned that Ma never ever parted from her husband. Having recognised her spiritual *Shakti*, he remained devoted to her till the very end of his life, and she too, kept up the promise she had made to her mother as a young girl: that she would love and serve her husband all her life. He was in government service; Ma went with him to Dhaka and other places when he was transferred; but wherever they went, he supported her spiritual *sadhanas*, and she was ever his faithful friend and mentor.

Gradually, Ma's fame began to spread. People who had heard about her intense spirituality and came to see her out of a sense of wonder and curiosity, stayed on to become her devoted disciples. They participated in *kirtan* sessions at her home; they were blessed enough to witness her going into spiritual ecstasy, in a state of *samadhi.*

A beautiful incident has been recorded by her devotees at this stage of her life. One day, Ma left her house in a trance during *kirtan*; she made her way in the darkness of the evening, to a small mosque in a by lane; she let herself in and walked into the shrine, reciting verses from the Holy Koran aloud. The caretaker of the mosque was stunned! He followed her back to her house and participated in the *kirtan*, with tears flowing from his eyes.

The strange thing was that Ma had never ever read the Koran or even heard it recited before that day!

The name Anandamayi Ma was given to her by her devotees in the 1920s to describe what they saw as her habitual state of divine joy and bliss.

From 1927 onwards Anandamayi Ma, as she was now called, began travelling extensively through India, accompanied by a few close devotees. It is said that she never stayed in any one place for more than two weeks. Once Mahatma Gandhi, who was a great admirer of Ma, asked her, "Why do you wander around so much?" her reply was simple: "This world is a garden of God; I only wander about this garden!"

Very often, going into a mood of ecstasy, Ma felt she was in the company of the deities and ancient sages. Rama and Krishna seemed to be near her, in their childhood forms. Devotees who were with her at such times, felt the thrill of God's presence in her company. She soon began to attract large gatherings around her. Abstruse scholars posed metaphysical questions to her; she answered them with absolute clarity and simplicity. People came to her with problems and miseries of life; she offered them comfort and hope. Spiritual seekers from the West heard of her and came to her; she welcomed them with love and grace.

Her husband Bholanath passed away in May 1938. During his last illness Ma was constantly by his bedside. He died with her hand on his head. But there was no sign of grief in Ma. To her devotees who looked at her in astonishment Ma merely said, "Do you start to wail and cry if a person goes to another room in the house? This death is inevitably connected with this life. In the sphere of Immortality, where is the question of death and loss? Nobody is lost to me."

Her fame spread far and wide. Wherever she went, her devotees established *ashrams* and temples. Twenty-five *ashrams* are named after her today. She also renovated many dilapidated holy places, including Naimisharanya, where she set up a temple and arranged for the recitation of holy names and the performance of *kirtan* and other religious rites. ParamahansaYogananda and Swami Sivananda met her and expressed their profound admiration for her. Kamala Nehru became an ardent devotee, and Indira Gandhi was an admirer of Ma from childhood. The Sadhu Samaj which was till then completely a male preserve, welcomed her into their fold as a truly Realised Soul.

Anandamayi Ma lived the life of an ascetic. She ate very little. Sometimes, she would eat practically nothing, for days together. At other times, she would only eat on alternate days. When people complained that she was not eating enough, Ma said, "It is not necessary to eat at all to preserve the body. I eat only because a semblance of normal behavior must be kept up so that you should not feel uncomfortable with me."

Ma never ever wrote or preached; her teachings have come down to us in the form of conversations and question-answers transcribed by devoted disciples. She did not urge her followers to follow any one prescribed method. "How can one impose limitations on the infinite by declaring *this is the only path*—and, why should there be so many different religions and sects? Because through every one of them He gives Himself to Himself, so that each person may advance according to his inborn nature."

ParamhansaYogananda recounts his meeting with her in his book, *Autobiography of a Yogi*. He calls her "The Bengali 'Joy-Permeated Mother'", and this is how she explains her background to him:

"Father, there is little to tell." She spread her graceful hands in a deprecatory gesture. "My consciousness has never associated itself with this temporary body. Before I came on this earth, Father, I was the same. As a little girl, I was the same. I grew into womanhood, but still I was the same. When

the family in which I had been born made arrangements to have this body married, I was the same... And, Father, in front of you now, I am the same. Ever afterward, though the dance of creation changes around me in the hall of eternity, I shall be the same."

Ma left for her heavenly abode on August 27, 1982 in Dehradun. She was later given her final *Samadhi* in the courtyard of her Kankhal *ashram*, near Haridwar. Today, a shrine known as the "Ananda Jyoti Peetham" stands over her Samadhi.

Anatomy, physiology and neurology can tell us about the body; but even modern psychology has not progressed enough to help us understand the human mind in all its complexity. As for what lies beyond the mind – western science and knowledge have no means to unravel the mysteries of the *atman*. This is where Hindu culture and tradition score over all the rest.

The body is strong; the senses (*indriyas*) are powerful. But the mind (*manas*) is above them. Beyond and higher than the mind is the discriminatory faculty (*buddhi*) that helps us know right from wrong and beyond it all is the *atman* – the Spirit.

Truly, every young man will evolve into a wonderful citizen, when he realises the need to conquer the enemy within, by means of *atmabalam* or spiritual strength. This awareness is reached, when he becomes aware of the power of the spirit! No man's life can be complete or truly happy, unless there is spiritual growth. And it is the woman in his life who can bring about this transformation.

Observing that judiciary and legislation alone cannot curb crimes, Rajya Sabha member M. Rama Jois, stressed the need for including spirituality in the education system to guide the youth properly towards success in life and mould them into law-abiding citizens.

"What does law do? It punishes the offenders. It cannot comprehensively prevent crimes that are manifestations of the uncontrolled human mind. We need a paradigm shift in our education system if we have to usher in reform in society, change the mind-set of male-dominated society," the former Punjab and Haryana High Court Chief Justice said.

Jois was addressing delegates at the International Conference on *Yoga, Ayurveda* and Spirituality (ICYAS), 2013.

"In case we have an education system that imbibes the values of *dharma*, respect for elders and women from elementary schools, crime level will come down naturally. In the process, *yoga* and spirituality will ensure the right to happiness of an individual," he said.

The Rajya Sabha MP lamented that many sections of society misunderstood the concept of *"dharma"*.

"*Dharma* is not connected to any particular religion. It purely refers to the code of conduct of an individual. Had we included *dharma* in our education system, we would not be witnessing such deterioration of values in society, including rapes and outraging modesty of women," he said.

Sead Avdic, Ambassador of Bosnia and Herzegovina to India, commended India's contribution to world peace.

"India is the mother of civilisation and culture...It should restore the world order by promoting its values of spirituality, peace and non-violence," he said.

– Courtesy: PTI

For Your Reflection

I say to all women: Our deepest fear is not that we are inadequate. Our deepest fear is that we are powerful beyond measure. It is our light, not our darkness that most frightens us. We ask ourselves, "Who am I to be brilliant, gorgeous, talented, fabulous?" Actually, who are you not to be? You are a child of God. Your playing small does not serve the world. There is nothing enlightened about shrinking so that other people won't feel insecure around you. We are all meant to shine, as children do. We were born to make manifest the glory of God that is within us. It's not just in some of us; it's in everyone. And as we let our own light shine, we unconsciously give other people permission to do the same. As we are liberated from our own fear, our presence automatically liberates others.

– **Marianne Williamson**

In our Bharatavarsha, woman is given a very high position and is worshipped as a Goddess. She is the progenitor of the Universe. She is the Shakti *or Energy without which even Shiva cannot create anything. ... an embodiment of patience, gentleness, softness, sweetness, service and ahimsa. It is the woman of India who has preserved the spiritual character of our society...*

— Dr. Sita Nambiar Mataji

The Sanskrit word Shakti *can be translated as meaning "power" or "energy". It is derived from the* parasmaipada *verb root "shak", which means "to be able", "to do", "to act". This power is witnessed in all the various phenomena of life. It is the force responsible for the growth of vegetation, animals and human beings. It is what is responsible for the movement of all things. The planets revolve around the sun as a result of* Shakti. *It is* Shakti *that makes the winds blow and the oceans churn.* Shakti *is manifest as the very effective ability of all the forces of nature. She is the heat of fire, the brilliance of the sun, the very life force of all living beings. In human beings, she is seen as the power of intelligence* (buddhi), *compassion* (daya) *and Divine love* (bhakti), *among her many other functions...*

— Sharma and Goswami

Chapter 16
Shakti

The one great need of our troubled world in this age of deepening darkness is the power of the spirit. Gurudev Sadhu Vaswani often said to us, "In the chaos and disorder of these days, in a world marred and mangled, a broken and blood-stained world, I say to all whom my voice may reach: 'Go to God; and He is not from you afar; He is within you'."

God is the secret, the hidden source of the *shakti* within us! "God is the secret of man," Gurudev Sadhu Vaswani asserted. He would have agreed that it is women who realise the truth of this hidden *shakti* that is within all of us!

JOAN OF ARC

In a small village called Domremy, in the province of Lorraine, in France, a girl child was born to Jacques and Isabelle d'Arc, on January 6, in the year 1412. Her father was a humble farmer, who provided for his family by cultivating the land which belonged to him.

It was a time of strife and unrest in France. There was an ugly civil war within France, between pro-British and anti-British factions of the French aristocracy. In this confusion, the English army invaded France. The disunited French army was no match for the determined English aggressors. Within a few years, treacherous French factions allowed King Henry V of England to be crowned the Monarch of France. It was an act of unprecedented shame and betrayal in the history of France. It was against the background of this bitter feud, that the stage was set for Joan to evolve into sainthood and martyrdom.

Joan grew up on her father's farm, a simple peasant girl. There was no school in Domremy, so she did not receive formal education. She went about the farm and village merrily; she laughed and played with other children; and like all the pious catholics of the village, she attended the church service every Sunday, without fail.

Around 1424, when she was 12, Joan began to have visions of the Saints Catherine and Margaret (two early Christian martyrs), and St. Michael, the Archangel who is described in the Bible as the Commander of God's army against Satan. As a child, these visions had merely instructed her to "be good and pious" and to "go to church regularly"; but over the next several years they had persistently called for her to stop the French defeat at the hands of the English; more specifically, she was asked to go to the Royal Court, and meet the dethroned French prince, the heir to the throne, who was living in Orleans, besieged by the English, in a hopeless condition, and to put him back on the throne of France!

Now, Joan finally decided that she would obey her 'voices'. She rushed to the nearest garrison town, and asked the local commander to provide her with an escort to go and meet her "Sovereign", Charles VII. She was provided with an escort, and, dressed in the clothes and armour of a typical soldier, she left for Orleans. As for the soldiers, they thought she was an angel in a girl's form. Firmly accepting her male attire for her personal safety and protection, Joan called herself 'La Pucelle' or The Maiden, and bravely travelled with her brother soldiers. They guarded her with their lives, and safely escorted her through war-ravaged districts to meet the prince.

Arriving at the court of the Dauphin in exile, she announced: "Most illustrious Lord Dauphin [i.e., heir to the throne], I have been sent in the Name of God to bring aid to you, and to put you back on the French throne."

To say that Charles and his courtiers were taken aback by this declaration, would be an understatement. But, Joan was determined to obey her voices; and indeed, the courtiers were half skeptical, half convinced, when she told them about her "voices".

Here was a theological problem, which had to be solved before they could accept any help from Joan. How could God or His representatives, the saints and angels, speak to Joan directly? After all, the Church was the intermediary between God and the people, and only through a priest of the church, could God 'speak' to ordinary mortals. How come, He had chosen to communicate directly to this peasant girl?

Charles sent her to Poitiers, where she was questioned by the French clergy for three weeks. This simple peasant girl held own against the learned theologians and earned a reputation as "another Saint Catherine come down to earth". This reputation began to spread. The clergy recommended that she should be given command of an army to obey the voices of the angels that she had heard.

Now began a remarkable phase of Joan's life. Clad in the resplendent armour of a commander, she went as the head of the French army, determined to lift and break the English siege of Orleans. She actually led the soldiers to the battlefront, though she did not participate in the fight. She carried the French banner aloft, and mingled with the fighting soldiers. She said that she would never carry weapons, but she did not want to be away from the dangers her soldiers faced. She constantly chanted God's Name and encouraged the soldiers to fight for God and their country.

When she was away from the actual battle, she exhorted the soldiers to go to church regularly; she urged them to say their prayers without fail; she beseeched them to lead a life of self-discipline and stay away from all forms of vice. For good measure, she also told them to give up swearing, and refrain from looting or harassing the innocent civilian population.

Cynics laughed her to scorn; but astonishingly, the defeated, demoralised, ordinary soldiers of the ravaged French Army, accepted her requests as if they were the diktat of their military commander. What appealed to them most, indeed, touched their hearts, was that she always spoke to them in the Name of God. The word began to spread that a saint was now at the head of the French army.

Miraculously, it seemed, the siege of Orleans was lifted. The arrogant English army, which, up to then, had faced no opposition worth the name, were stunned and shocked. The lifting of the siege of Orleans was a shot in the arm of French Royalists. The Dauphin was overjoyed, and proclaimed that he would now do whatever Joan wanted him to do. Joan had only one goal: to crown him the King of France, as his ancestors had been crowned, in Rheims Cathedral.

Now, Joan personally ordered the placement of the troops, and decided on matters of strategy. Some of the captains were jealous and suspicious of her growing influence; but others recognised her divine powers, and saluted the indomitable spirit of courage and patriotism that she brought with her; and what is more, she managed to infuse the same into the soldiers.

Joan's dream was accomplished soon. After a series of spectacular defeats inflicted on the English, the French troops advanced towards Rheims. On July 17, 1429, at last the Dauphin was crowned King of France, with Joan leading his cheering courtiers. Her mission had been accomplished!

What followed this triumph was unfortunate: trials and tribulations confronted Joan. Her voices warned her, that before long, she would be captured and betrayed. And so it proved to be. The English army had regrouped and realigned their strategy; and they had a one point agenda now: to capture the Maid alive, and burn her at the stake as a heretic. French treachery and English hatred worked against the Maid. As if this were not enough, the orthodox clergy of the Church also condemned her as a serious heretic, for she had dared to claim direct communion with God, sidestepping the mediation of the Church and its priests. Without exception, all her enemies felt that Joan represented a dangerous trend which had to be eliminated at all costs!

Joan was captured by the treacherous Burgundyan faction, and made a prisoner of the English garrison. An ecclesiastical trial – the infamous Inquisition – was set up, to try her as a heretic. They wanted to excommunicate her, and burn her at the stake – the typical punishment accorded to those who dared to defy the Church in the Medieval Ages.

She was accused of witchcraft; her voices were dismissed as devilish; her saints were declared to be demons in disguise. It was nothing but a kangaroo court which indicted an innocent girl on trumped up charges. She was pronounced a heretic and handed over to the English forces. They, in their wisdom, decided that she would be burnt at the stake.

The scene of her execution is vividly described by a number of those who were present that day. She listened calmly to the sermon read to her, but then broke down weeping during her own address, in which she forgave her accusers for what they were doing and asked them to pray for her. She asked for a cross, which one sympathetic English soldier tried to provide by making a small one out of wood. A crucifix was brought from the nearby church and a Friar from Rome held it up in front of her until the flames rose.

Several eyewitnesses recalled that she repeatedly screamed "in a loud voice the holy name of Jesus, and implored and invoked without ceasing the aid of the saints of Paradise". Then her head drooped, and it was over.

Joan had been martyred. Joan had been burnt to death as a heretic. But Joan's spirit triumphed. The Church realised that its officers had erred grievously against truth and the French people's sentiments. Posthumously, a retrial was ordered in which Joan was vindicated and her accusers denounced. The Church subsequently declared Joan a martyr, thereby paving the way for her eventual beatification in 1909 and canonization as a saint in 1920.

Joan is revered today as "the Maid of Orleans" and the national heroine of France. At the very spot where she was burnt, stands a magnificent statue of the Maid, in those very soldier's garbs, which she was condemned for wearing. The wheel has turned full circle!

In his quiet but tremendously influential work among youth and women, Gurudev Sadhu Vaswani's emphasis was on *shakti*. His aspiration was to build a "school of *shakti*" for the service of India and the world. He founded the *Shakti Ashram* at Rajpur for this purpose. It was to awaken this tremendous *shakti* within women that he founded at first the *Sakhi Satsang*, and later, the MIRA Movement in Education.

Gurudev Sadhu Vaswani was a visionary who believed that women had a great potential – a great *shakti* – which could be utilised for the betterment of the society and the nation. It was not long before the enlightened people of Hyderabad (Sind) began to appreciate the service being rendered to the community by Gurudev Sadhu Vaswani's devoted disciples. A number of men who were inspired by the Master begged him to permit them to join his *satsang*. The Master graciously consented and the *satsang* and its activities were open to all. This was how the *Sakhi Satsang* now became the Brotherhood Association.

Many of us mistakenly equate *shakti* with power or force. And power is always associated with masculine energy. But the Hindu way of thinking is different. In the *Sanatana Dharma*, *shakti* is essentially the feminine principle, the Goddess or *Devi* as she is worshipped by millions.

It is not without reason that every major deity in the Hindu pantheon has His own consort or *Shakti*. She represents his 'better', kinder, more compassionate half. *Shakti* worshippers believe that without Her, He has no power. It is *Shakti* who uses Her intuitive feminine powers to bring balance to the world. *Shakti* is also the Divine force that helps in destroying demonic forces. *Shakti* compliments the masculine and provides a sense of balance. Indeed, She is the inherent power in all things, the primordial manifest being, the Cosmic Principle of Life.

The Divine image of Shiva as *Ardhanarishwara* represents this ideal – of the Divinity as half Male and half Female. This image symbolises the affinity and unity between the two principles, which may be opposed in visual appearance, but are nevertheless indivisible and function in harmony in each act of the creation. They are two aspects of the same being, both to be adored and venerated as much as the other. I must add here, that it is not without significance that every woman in India is seen as a manifestation of this Divine Principle, *Shakti*.

The distinguished Western scholar, Dr. Frank Gaetano Morales, Ph.D. observes: "As the twenty-first century begins, we find ourselves entering an era in which the more feminine qualities of compassion, nurturing, tolerance and love are rapidly replacing the outmoded anthropomorphic notion of God as a judgmental and vengeful old man in the sky so prevalent in the Abrahamic religions." He adds words of great significance to this concept: "In *Sanatana Dharma*, the dual issues of respecting the ways of nature and respecting women are ultimately inseparable concerns."

Dr. Morales points out that though the *Shakti* Concept provides a truly visionary framework for the true liberation of women; it has been misinterpreted or misrepresented by some feminists, who have deliberately chosen to reject the positive and life-enhancing qualities of the feminine aspect of human nature – and especially the spiritual dimension of the feminine.

May I say to you, *shakti* is not merely a force; *shakti* is integration, in the truest sense of that term. Today, disintegration is setting in.

RANI LAXMIBAI OF JHANSI

The very name Jhansi Ki Rani is an inspiration to Indian women. Queen of the princely state of Jhansi, this brave and spirited lady became one of the greatest legends of the Indian War of Independence in the nineteenth century. Even today, she stands as a symbol of resistance to colonial rule, and is referred to lovingly as "India's own Joan of Arc".

Born in a pious and learned Brahmin family and married to the Raja of Jhansi at whose court her father was a minister, Laxmibai was more independent than most women of her age; she was well-trained in equestrian skills, archery and self-defence. Not content with training herself, she also trained a group of women in her court, in the martial arts, to form her own women's army.

When her husband passed away at an untimely age, it was left to Rani Laximbai to keep her beloved Jhansi comparatively calm, peaceful and secure – this, at a time, when the British empire in India was literally being shaken by the unprecedented sepoy mutiny, which is now called the First War of Indian Independence.

When the British decided to lay a siege to Jhansi, Rani Laxmibai and her followers decided not to surrender. She rallied her troops together, strengthened the fortifications of the city, and fought fiercely. Though Jhansi was captured, she managed to escape with her faithful band of women soldiers, to regroup her resistance movement against the British in the neighbouring Kingdom of Gwalior. This great woman of remarkable beauty, courage and intelligence, died a brave warrior's death, fighting the enemy until her last breath.

"Main Meri Jhansi Nahi Doongi!" I will never, ever give up my Jhansi!

This brave cry still echoes and re-echoes in the hearts of all Indians, and the brave and heroic woman who gave that clarion call, has become one of the icons of the Indian Independence Movement. She is indeed, a symbol and inspiration to the concept of women's empowerment.

Woman, who is the centre of social integration, can stem the tide that threatens to destabilise our society. To reassert Gurudev Sadhu Vaswani's claim: "The woman-soul has the *shakti* to rebuild the shattered world on the strength of her intuitions, her purity, her simplicity, her spiritual aspirations, her sympathy and silent sacrifice. The woman-soul will lead us upward, on!"

Consider Sita; the delicate princess who followed her beloved Rama into *vanvaas* with a smile on her lips; Sita who defied the mighty Ravana even in captivity. Consider Maitreyi, who rejected her husband's offer of material wealth and comfort and insisted instead, that he should share his wealth of wisdom and spiritual knowledge with her. Consider Mira, who rejected social conventions and gave up the life of a queen to seek Krishna. Indian scriptures, epics and history stand testimony to the greatness of the woman soul.

Given this background, it is sad that what we are witnessing today is a detrimental movement away from this concept of the sacred feminine.

Vandana Shiva, the environmental activist and eco feminist tells us: "The violence to nature as symptomatised by the ecological crisis, and the violence to women, as symptomitised by their subjugation and exploitation, arise from this subjugation of the feminine principle."

I read an ancient Greek story about a city that was threatened by an awesome mythical monster, called the Unicorn. The warriors and other brave men of the city could not stand up to the monster and fled in disarray. But a pure, simple, virtuous young maiden confronted the monster – and it was the monster that had to flee from the *shakti* that she represented.

I find this story deeply symbolic.

For our world today is threatened by the nameless, faceless monster that is compounded of hatred, violence, intolerance, insensitivity, ruthlessness and avarice. It is only the woman – pure, gentle, virtuous, strong in the spirit of simplicity, service and sacrifice, who can take on the monster and conquer him with her spiritual *shakti*.

India's greatest attribute is the pluralistic nature of its tradition. Hindus, the majority community, have multiple myths and have multi-faceted icons. Those who talk about "Sita's fate" for girls crossing the "*Lakshman Rekha*" should also mull over the concept of *Ardhanarishwara*, which represents the synthesis of masculine and feminine energies of the universe and which illustrates how *Shakti*, the female principle of God, is inseparable from Shiva, the male principle of God. India's myths and traditions offer us many pathways – it is up to us to decide whether we stay with the patriarchal strand or embrace the more inclusive ones.

– Courtesy: DNA

For Your Reflection

What is true on the macrocosmic level is also the rule on the microcosmic. Human beings too are said to participate in the interplay of *shakti* and *shaktiman*. For in Hinduism, every woman is said to be a manifestation of the Divine *Shakti*. The power of *Shakti*, the feminine principle, is believed to be directly present in creation in the form of our mothers, sisters, daughters and wives. As the contemporary feminist author Elinor Gadon explains, "The truth of the Goddess is the mystery of our being. She is the dynamic life force within. Her form is embedded in our collective psyche..."

– Frank Morales, *The Concept of Shakti: Hinduism as a Liberating Force for Women*

Chapter 17
Dada Answers Questions By women, On women, For women

Q: Why are women the oppressed class in most parts of the world?

Ans: The world functions by very different yardsticks at different times in history. There was a time when in India women were worshipped as Goddesses. In those days, people had respect for the scriptures and respect for values. Today, the three things people value most are money, pleasure and power. In many parts of the world, women are still comparatively less educated and are unable to occupy powerful positions and draw fat salaries. This probably explains the oppression and neglect you speak of. However, times are changing. One to one, women are capable of handling authority, responsibility, leadership and administration and also capable of earning more money than men, if they set their hearts to it. Women who make it to the Forbes Fortune 500 are talked about. Women who figure in the top ten of the world's most powerful people are looked up to! It is these things that matter in the eyes of the world! I believe the day is not far off when women will be held in high respect for all the right reasons.

Q: Why do men feel superior to women? Or, ridicule women?

Ans: It is social conditioning over the generations, that has led to this attitude in some men – please take note, I said "some men", because many men think differently. As things are now, might is right, and men have the upper hand. They wield more power and resources than women do. But as I have said earlier, times are changing.

Q: What attributes should a woman look for in a man while choosing a life partner?

Ans: Many young women today have their personal preferences and look for different attributes. If any of them were to ask me, I would recommend the following:

He should have love for God and fear of displeasing God.

He should be courteous and civil, and have respect for culture and values.

He should have the capacity to earn enough and a little more to be able to bring up a family.

He should be a man of understanding – humble, gentle, and full of the spirit of helpfulness, forgiveness.

He must have a sense of humour, otherwise life can be painful.

He should be able to control his temper and be quick to forgive.

Q: What are your views on dating? Should a girl date before making the final selection?

Ans: Even if I suggest that there should be no dating, no one will listen to me. So let them date, but let them not be carried away during the period of courtship. There is nothing better than self-discipline and the wisdom to draw one's own boundaries. If you follow this ideal, there can be nothing wrong with dating.

I am told that some people date multiple partners before they finally choose one with whom they wish to pursue their relationship. In such cases, you have to exercise extra caution. Dating cannot become an excuse for continuous flirting with many members of the opposite sex.

Men are at their best when they are wooing. But immediately after marriage, many of them take their brides for granted and pay scant attention to them. It is during this period of courtship that women should ensure that men understand them and also teach them to be genuinely caring and sensitive. Perhaps they should also extract promises from their fiancés to become what every sensitive woman would want them to be.

Q: What are your views on divorce?

Ans: I believe in the Law of *Karma*. It is their *karma* that brings a couple together in wedlock. In many cases one spouse has to settle accounts with the other, pending from previous births! This is what I understand to be the real meaning of the saying, *Marriages are made in heaven*! We are fulfilling our *karmic* debts, reaping our *karmic* obligations through marriage. Marriage is meant for two partners to evolve together spiritually. Therefore, I do not believe in divorce. I feel it is better to pay our *karmic* debts off than to accumulate them and pay later with interest.

Q: What quality or qualities should women develop to become complete?

Ans: Women are the repositories of several worthy qualities. Today, I feel they need to develop more courage, self-confidence and self-esteem. They must also learn to count their blessings, and cultivate the love of silence, patience and punctuality; when necessary, they must also know how to shrug their shoulders and say very firmly to themselves, "It is none of my business." (This is, when they tend to interfere in matters that do not concern them personally or socially.) Mind you, these are qualities that all of us need to develop!

Q: What is the one advice you would give a newly wedded couple?

Ans: Avoid the next quarrel and perchance if you do quarrel, don't let the sun set on your quarrel.

Q: Certain negative emotions are more obviously pre-dominant in women. Even though they are aware of these harmful emotions they cannot overcome them. These are jealousy, pride and vanity. How can they be overcome?

Ans: Men too, have their negative traits like greed, aggression and anger. All of us can overcome our negative traits with the grace of the Guru and God. Whosoever wishes to overcome these negative emotions should pray without ceasing and she will soon see the result.

Q: What advice would you give to new-age mothers who strive to make their kids super-heroes?

Ans: I am afraid I don't have get-smart-quick tricks to share with you! But I do recommend a time tested method that mothers have used from times immemorial. Mothers should relate to their kids the life-stories of great souls – men and women who have not hesitated to sacrifice their all at the altar of God, in service of fellow human beings who travail in suffering and pain. You see, I think children today are born smart, and get even smarter as they grow up. The training of their heads is well taken care of. Mothers must therefore focus attention on training the hearts of the children, by giving them the right values and inculcating the finer virtues like care and compassion.

Q: What are your views on pre-marital relationships?

Ans: My view on such new fads is strictly non-negotiable! You might find my views conservative or old-fashioned. But it is my firm belief that pre-marital relations are the beginning of the end of society.

Q: Should living in joint families be encouraged?

Ans: Children who grow up with two or three older generations tend to be more humane, courteous, caring and selfless. I think that as things stand today, many young parents are finding that grandparents are the best people to care for children, and that they are also the most trusted and loving 'child minders'. This is one selfish reason which is prompting many Indians in Western countries to take their parents to live with them. Therefore, yes, I do believe that joint families should be encouraged. It is beneficial on many counts: it ensures that we care for our elders, that our children are well cared for, and it also takes the stress off young couples and parents.

But let me say to you, it is people, especially women, who can make or mar joint families. A despotic older woman or intransigent younger woman (mother-in-law or daughter-in-law) can nullify all the advantages I have listed! This is why I recommend that we have mothers-in-love and daughters-in-love instead of 'in-laws' as they are usually referred.

Q: Given people's propensity for independence and privacy, isn't it hard to live in a joint family?

Ans: The kind of desire for freedom you speak of is illusory and short-lived! When the reality of routine life starts and the glamour of early marriage romance wears off, the presence of elders in the home can prove to be invaluable. The advantages of living in a joint family are manifold, chief among them being that the children will grow in the love and fear of God and in those qualities of character which alone give a meaning and significance to life. And youngsters can have no idea how comforting and supportive it is to have elders to turn to, in times of trouble and crisis. But there should be mutual understanding between the elders and the youngsters.

Q: Every day we hear cases about rape, violence against women and wife-battering as it is called in the west (domestic violence). Even in big cities, women are victims of heinous crimes and atrocities. Why do so many girls and women suffer for no fault of their own? We know that many of them are absolutely innocent.

Ans: It is very difficult to answer this question. Perhaps one answer could be that according to the Law of *Karma* previous accounts are being settled. But the men who indulge in such atrocities are creating terrible consequences for themselves through negative *karma*.

Let me make it clear that I do not condone or justify the atrocities we have been discussing on the grounds of *karma!* But *karma* and free will are like two arms of a pair of scissors. Those of us who indulge in such acts of atrocity will pay the price, perhaps manifold, sooner or later. As for the victims, though our hearts go out to them in grief and sorrow, we must learn to look at them with greater understanding, as members of a society which is collectively responsible for whatever has happened. There is no use pointing fingers at them or blaming them for what happened. The focus should be on swift punishment, deterrent measures and strict laws for the offenders; and humane treatment, safety, security and quick justice for the victims.

Q: Why are women always expected to sacrifice?

Ans: As I have said earlier in this book, sacrifice is a universal ideal that all of us must practice! But still, there are certain things that women can do more easily than men. One of them is selfless sacrifice. Obviously, it cannot happen under compulsion!

Child-bearing, child-rearing, home-making, even cooking: there was a time when such acts were not thought of as sacrifices. But today, some women consider them as a burden they have to bear. They have a choice, like the rest of us! But I cannot help thinking that the role of a woman entails selflessness and sacrifice.

Q: Are you saying that they have to keep on sacrificing? Why it is considered the duty of a girl to compromise and make sacrifices in her life as a daughter, as a wife, as a mother, as a home-maker and even as a career woman?

Ans: Because this is a man made world. Now women will rise and we will have a woman made world, a woman-made civilisation. Then things will change. But I appeal to my sisters, be kind to men. Kindness is your special quality — kindness, compassion, love and sympathy. Don't give up those qualities.

Q: Is it important for every girl to get married even if she is not in favour of it?

Ans: I have the greatest respect in the world for the married state or *grihasta ashrama* as it is referred to in our scriptures. But I don't think girls (or boys) should be forced into marriage if they are not for it. Biologically it is necessary for some people — boys or girls to marry; but it is not necessary for all. And now that we have an explosion of population, it will become worse if every body marries.

Q: What should a wife do to keep her relationship strong in this world of temptations?

Ans: She should pray for her husband everyday and give him a little more freedom. It is said they asked George Bernard Shaw what was the best birthday present he could expect from his wife. He smiled and answered, "Once a year she can give me a little more freedom to meet other women I like."

Someone has also said the best couple in the world is a blind man and a deaf woman! The man will not have a 'roving eye' which wives hate, and the woman will not retort and talk back constantly – something husbands are allergic to.

Jokes apart, the best thing that husbands and wives can do to keep their love fresh is to cultivate greater understanding and appreciation for each other.

Q: Do you think we need to have a stricter dress code for young girls and women?

Ans: Do we have a dress code for young men or older men? Since the answer is 'No', I don't see any logic in insisting on a dress code for women.

Men and women attend our daily *satsang* at the Sadhu Vaswani Mission. We do not prescribe a dress code for them. But we do expect them to come dressed with decency and dignity. If each of us exercises these rules of self-discipline, why would a dress code be necessary? If you are comfortable wearing certain clothes, and your clothes do not get you unwanted attention or unwelcome stares, isn't that something you would prefer?

That, of course, is with regard to your personal life. It is best determined by the context and the situation you are in. I doubt if any woman in her bridal finery will walk to the nearest bus stop to catch a bus. Nor is a man in a bathrobe likely to go out to buy his morning newspaper. We dress differently to go to meetings, parties, picnics or places of worship. But sensible people don't call attention to themselves by wearing outlandish or abnormal clothes.

Educational institutions and workplaces insist on their own dress code and people normally observe these codes. Many executives I meet tell me that Western wear like closed neck shirts, ties and jackets, can be very uncomfortable in India, especially during the hot weather. They have evolved a formal, but less constricting form of office wear to suit their corporate culture. It is a combination of what is appropriate and what is convenient.

Q: India is increasingly becoming an unsafe place to live. Can you tell us how we can make it a safer place to live for all of us?

Ans: May I say to you, it is not just in India, but the world is passing through a period in which discipline is conspicuous by its absence. We are reading that in America, little boys carrying pistols in their hands are shooting their own grandmothers. Just imagine! We could never have imagined this twenty or thirty years ago. But such things are happening all over the world now. It is not only India that is unsafe, it is the world that has become unsafe. Probably that is why they are trying to sell space on the moon and people are purchasing space on the moon. They think perhaps that they will be safer there.

How can we make India a safe place? I think we need a new type of education. The education that we are giving to our students now is only an education in words. We need a new education for life, not just for livelihood. Students need to be taught how to speak the truth though the heavens fall. Students need to be taught how to develop their energies and spend them in the service of the surrounding world. Students need to be taught, how to live unselfish lives. Our education teaches young people how to become competitive, to win at all costs, it encourages them to become more and more selfish. The worth of the student who passes out of a course is determined by the salary he is paid! Everybody wants to get a higher salary than the other.

So I say to you, let us start from the basics, if we are to make India a safer place. Let us give our children a new type of education — an education which should teach the students that life is larger than livelihood, that the end of knowledge is not jobs and careers, not gains in silver and gold but service and sacrifice. What is needed is a life of discipline. We need to inculcate discipline in the students, so that they may grow up to be responsible citizens of this country, who will not threaten the peace and harmony of the social fabric.

If we had discipline, we would have no traffic violations, no tax evasions, no frauds and forgeries, no corruption, no crimes!

Q: Do you think that rape should be punishable by death?

Ans: I have said time and again, that I do not believe in the death penalty, for the simple reason that we can't take away that which we cannot give back to a person. Rape, like murder and torture, is a heinous offence. But the emphasis should be on prevention and deterrence. Deterrent punishment, yes; death penalty, no. Not just human rights groups, but even women's organisations rejected the death penalty as an option when their opinions were sought by the recent Varma Commission enquiries.

Having said that, it is a sad state of affairs the world over, where very few rapists serve their full term in jail, which might be life or 11-15 years. Prison statistics in the US and Australia reveal that most offenders get away with bail before even half their terms are completed, while some get away with suspended sentences.

I am no expert on these matters, but I can see the wisdom of experts who recommend that implementation of existing penalties and stricter policing would be the best ways to prevent these heinous crimes.

But I feel very strongly that such offenders should be given life imprisonment so that people know that they cannot play with our richest gift, for the richest treasure of India has been the purity of our women. No woman should be molested. This is really the most heinous crime that a person can indulge in. It is only with such punishment that you can bring about the desired change among the offenders.

Q: Do you think women should be trained in self-defense and martial arts?

Ans: I think this is absolutely essential and should be taken up by our schools and colleges on a war footing. Most crimes against women happen because they are physically weaker and cannot stand up to the brute and animal force of the criminals. I would urge all women to develop physical and mental strength, so that they can escape the vicious clutches of fear and insecurity.

Q: Dada, how can we change people's minds towards the girl child?

Ans: I think a period will come when people realise that it is better to have a girl child than a boy child! We all know the proverb, "My son is a son till I get him a wife, but my daughter is my daughter for the rest of her life!" When boys grow up they don't think of their parents. But as girls grow up, they like to serve their parents. So I think gradually this change will come about, in people's hearts. People would like to have girl children and not just boys. But let me also say to you, the parents are more worried about their girls. Society is so made that parents worry about the safety and future of their daughters. This is one of the reasons why they still prefer boys. But all that will change.

Q: What do you think are the reasons for gender inequality?

Ans: If you look at our history, you will understand that India has been enslaved by too many foreign invaders. The foreigners imposed certain restrictions on women which men were not subject to. Women had to stay at home; women were not sent out to be educated; women could not go out without being fully covered; women could not inherit property and so on. This led to constant and continuous degeneration of the status of women in society. But the time has come when we must set this imbalance right, and this, as I said to you earlier, is possible only through the right type of education.

Let me reiterate: my hope is not in politics or legislation. My hope is in a new education that integrates the training of the head, hand and heart. This education should be inspired and guided by men and women of light and understanding, men and women of illumination.

Our education does nothing to train the heart, the higher emotions. Our education has only trained the brain, and brain power has indeed flourished. Technological progress has been made. Science is marching on. But the problems that are before the nation today, the problems that are before India today, will not be solved by developed brains alone. We need awakened hearts, illumined hearts.

Q: Dada, what should women do to safeguard their dignity and self-respect?

Ans: Women should become strong — physically, mentally, spiritually. If they do, men will not even think of troubling women. It is because they know that women are weak that they believe they can do whatever they like with them. Thus they take advantage, and they actually exploit and harass women, they even molest them.

I suggest that women should form guilds or groups and take up training in self defence techniques like Taekwondo and Karate. Each and every woman should become a veritable dynamo of strength so that men are afraid of approaching them or even looking at them in the wrong manner.

However much we say that might should not be right, I am sorry to say that might is becoming right today. It is only brute power that makes men treat women so badly. Now we have to face the situation and take matters into our own hands.

I am happy to tell you that self defence courses are offered to our girl students for the last 12 years at St. Mira's College, which has now become a model, a benchmark for training girls in self-defense.